THE WOMAN READER

Courses studying writing for, by and about women grew out of the women's movement of the 1970s, and have changed as feminism itself has developed over the past twenty years.

In *The Woman Reader*, Jean Milloy and Rebecca O'Rourke offer a practical guide for students and teachers of women's writing courses from the perspective of over ten years' experience in adult education.

While much feminist criticism has originated in academic institutions, Milloy and O'Rourke assert the relevance of studying women's writing to a wide range of women students, including those who have often been excluded from literary studies. They discuss various strategies for learning and teaching, and give an honest account of some of the mistakes and difficulties they have experienced, particularly as they moved towards an understanding of the workings of racism and heterosexism in the classroom. The book combines study of feminist thinking about questions of autobiography, differences of race and sexuality, women's writing and history with discussions of writers. It will be an invaluable resource for teachers and students of women's writing, as well as for librarians and others working in adult education.

Jean Milloy has worked as a basic education and adult education teacher. She is currently co-ordinator of an adult numeracy project in London.

Rebecca O'Rourke has taught women's writing and creative writing on a variety of adult education courses. She now combines lecturing with writing and reviewing.

THE WOMAN READER

Learning and Teaching Women's Writing

Jean Milloy and Rebecca O'Rourke

London and New York

First published 1991
by Routledge
11 New Fetter Lane, London EC4P 4EE

Simultaneously published in the USA and Canada
by Routledge
a division of Routledge, Chapman and Hall, Inc.
29 West 35th Street, New York, NY 10001

© 1991 Jean Milloy and Rebecca O'Rourke

Typeset in 10/12pt Bembo by
Falcon Typographic Art Ltd., Edinburgh & London
Printed in Great Britain by
Clays Ltd., St Ives plc, Suffolk

British Library Cataloguing in Publication Data
Milloy, Jean

The woman reader: learning and teaching women's writing.
1. Authorship
I. Title II. O'Rourke, Rebecca
808.02

Library of Congress Cataloging in Publication Data
Milloy, Jean
The woman reader: learning and teaching women's writing/
Jean Milloy and Rebecca O'Rourke.
p. cm.
Includes bibliographical references (p. 139) and index.
1. English literature – Women authors – Study and teaching.
2. American literature – Women authors – Study and teaching.
3. Feminism and literature – Study and teaching. 4. Women and
literature – Study and teaching. 5. Adult education of women –
Great Britain. 6. Women – Great Britain – Books and reading.
I. O'Rourke, Rebecca. II. Title.
PR119.M55   1991
820.9'9287'07—dc20   90–24229 CIP

ISBN 0 415 00983 9
ISBN 0 415 00984 7 pbk

CONTENTS

ACKNOWLEDGEMENTS

Many thanks to Irene Schwab for her help with the proofreading and her work in compiling the index.

The authors and publishers would like to thank Faber & Faber Ltd and Faber & Faber Inc. for permission to reproduce an extract from Sylvia Plath's *Collected Poems*.

INTRODUCTION

We have been teaching, separately and together, courses and work-shops that focus on women's writing for over ten years. Our experience covers adult basic education, Fresh Start and Return to Study, Workers' Educational Association (WEA) and Adult Education Institute (AEI) courses, further and higher education. Throughout, our aim has been to examine women's writing with groups of women and to explore both the ways in which that writing has changed and developed over time and particularly under the influence of the current wave of feminism, and the ways in which women themselves change and develop through reading and the discussion of writing.

Reading, like writing, is traditionally regarded as an isolated activity, occurring at home or in the study, in silence, separate, sometimes even operating as a shield against the rest of the world. Women have long been regarded as passive consumers of certain types of writing (fiction, particularly romantic, historical, glam-orous; biography and autobiography; magazines), and publishers have a notion of a 'women's market'. Over the last fifteen to twenty years this market has shifted significantly to include writing pub-lished by women's publishing houses, and commercial publishers have also launched women's lists and imprints.

This shift reflects gradual changes in attitudes to writing and to reading that have occurred through the impetus of the women's movement and developed partly through Women's Studies courses. Much of the feminist fiction and poetry published in Britain in the early to mid-1970s came out of women's writing groups (collec-tions like *Tales I Tell My Mother* and *Smile, Smile, Smile, Smile*, and novels like Michèle Roberts: *A Piece Of The Night*), and these workshops themselves were extensions of the consciousness-raising groups within which women learned to transcend the polemic derived from socialism into a woman-centred theory which draws on and fuels personal and political experience.

The drive behind this writing was the exploration and expression of women's lives and realities from within a women's context, with the initial reference points being oneself and one's women friends. This approach was both to provide a safe and supportive background to work in, and to create a solidarity from which to take critical stances against patriarchal society. And the implicit audience for this writing were women who were struggling with similar processes of development and thought. Thus it became possible to envisage women as a potential audience, not in the conventional manner of passive consumers, but as participants and contributors. Reading acquired positive connotations, and those aspects of women's writing that critics had always considered typical of women's work (attention to detail, a concern with the domestic and familial, love and romance) were transformed through recognition and identification into political statements and analyses.

It is these transformations that we seek to address in our courses and to describe in this book. Women writers have taken the process of writing as part of their subject-matter; women readers can construct a reading practice that enables them to respond to, criticise and celebrate women's writing. By centring the process of reading, by focusing on reading as an active and constructive process, we can take reading out of the private and into the public domain, and begin to develop a wide-ranging and non-elitist, feminist critical practice.

In this book we describe some of the courses we have presented. We have also emphasised the thinking that lay behind the courses, and the ways in which we and our students learned how to work together and make demands on each other. The chapters of the book vary in length. Some set out in detail our ideology and methodology for specific courses, including course plans, booklists, and accounts of the teaching and learning experience (for example, 'Senses of the Past' and 'Feminism and Writing'). Other chapters, such as 'Differences', and 'The Personal', contain more general and reflective overviews of themes and issues that permeated our own lives and thinking as well as those of our students. Such themes and issues, e.g. an increased awareness of racism generated both by the increasing anger of Black women and the spread of Equal Opportunities Policies, affected our teaching and the demands made on us by students.

We have organised the book in these two ways – the analytical and the synthetic – partly because this reflects changes in our own approaches and partly because we believe that both methods used in conjunction have real value. As individuals, we started from a view of the women's movement as prioritising the struggle against men and the patriarchy over all other differences. However, the differences between women are sometimes greater and more powerful than such a homogeneous view suggests. We feel we are now moving to a sense of women's struggle as being rooted in a variety of oppressions which women experience and challenge in different ways and from different standpoints. Some of this change has come from our work and interaction with students; some from other shifts and pressures (Clause 28; the New Racism; the Thatcherite view of the family).

Throughout the book we have tried to cite references and suggest activities that we have found useful and effective. Some themes, such as 'Mothers and Daughters' (which could fill a whole book on its own), have been subsumed to allow space for less familiar themes, such as 'Love, Sex and Friendship'. Sometimes we have emphasised specific sections of courses, such as students' exercises in criticism during the 'Love, Sex and Friendship' course, as this was a new departure for us and for the students. We have also examined work with groups at different levels, including basic education, as well as within the Workers' Educational Association and Adult Education Institutes.

We have tried in our writing to reflect the dynamic processes of teaching and learning, and to illustrate the challenging, stimulating and sometimes risky situations which are the essence of working with women. We hope that you will find the book helpful, and as inspiring as we found our classes.

1

FEMINISM AND WRITING

Although feminism is responsible for the Women's Studies courses we have, it is not always explicit within them. In our experience of teaching and learning in London, Birmingham, Middlesbrough and Manchester since the late 1970s, there seems to have been a marked decline in the willingness of women to identify themselves with feminism. Ten years ago, adult education classes in Women's Studies were as likely to attract students rooted in feminism, sometimes with experience of further or higher education, as they were women new to education and new to women's liberation. Feminism, as a topic but also as local action and campaigns, was a focal point for the whole class. There was a shared evangelism, a desire to bring feminism's truths and insights to a wider audience, to 'ordinary' women. We put 'ordinary' into quotation marks partly because it is a quotation, although from sources too numerous to record, and partly to indicate what a slippery term it is. 'Ordinary' can mean any number of things, often simultaneously.

It can mean women who are not yet feminists but not known to be overtly hostile to the feminist movement. Or women who are deeply suspicious of some aspects of feminism, which must be played down in order not to put them off. Old favourites here are lesbianism and anti-racism. It can mean working-class women or Black women. The women who actually grew up and live in the town you come to as a student. Married women. Women with children. Women who don't go to meetings. Women who don't want to be involved. Women active in their Trade Union. Women at home. Older women. Younger women.

Ordinary women were assumed to be out there waiting to be won over, shown the way. Given the books, the courses, the ideas, they would then flock to the cause, the meetings, the centres. It

1

didn't happen like that. The women's movement itself fragmented under the weight of claiming to speak for all women. At the same time, the Conservative Party primed the shift towards enterprise culture under the country's first woman prime minister. A series of policy changes gradually eroded women's opportunities in the public sector whilst championing an image of success open to anyone, male or female, Black or white, willing to work hard and risk it. Practically and ideologically feminists had a fight on their hands they were not equal to: a surge of power-dressed, high-achieving 1980s businesswomen swept them, and 'ordinary women' with them, under the carpet.

The world became post-feminist or it simply surged on, barely nodding a thank you to the women whose struggles had made possible the opportunities so eagerly exploited. The politics of the personal, for those still resisting the new-wave individualism and competitive spirit abroad, began to seem as hollowly self-indulgent as it had always been accused of being in the light of prolonged assaults, and victories, upon the civil and social liberty of the people of this country: the miners' strike and dozens of less glorified, less publicised disputes that were rattled down like ninepins; the abolition of the GLC and metropolitan counties; the reorganisation of the National Health Service, the Falklands war, GCHQ, Section 28 of the Local Government Act; rate capping; the deaths of children in the care of the Social Services; the Cleveland sexual abuse scandal; the abolition of protective housing legislation; the changes to eligibility for social security benefits; privatisation of nationalised industries and assets: water, gas, British Telecom, British Steel; disasters that speak eloquently of a cynical preference for profit over people: the herald of free enterprise indeed. And feminists, women who were actively, proudly grateful to be feminists, are left teaching courses on feminism as if it was a historical curiosity, as indeed, for some women, it is.

In 1984 we ran a nine-week course called 'The Position of the Feminist Writer'. We are now going to look back at that course, comparing what we did then with what we, or other tutors, might do now and discuss the kinds of issues courses in this general area raise. One of the most obvious is names. That first course of ours referred to 'the' feminist writer and, with the reading list's emphasis on the work of Michèle Roberts, suggested that feminist writers were few and far between. In 1984, this was not exactly stretching the truth. The greater part of feminist publishing then concentrated on reprints, either from abroad, usually America, or from the past. We also talked about 'the' position, as if that, too, was a fixed thing, although our actual approach explored the variety of viewpoints on feminism and writing. Names too are a way of signalling who the course is aimed at particularly and specifying its concerns. 'An introduction to . . .' 'An exploration of . . .' indicate a more preliminary sort of course than issues in . . . would. A subtitle would make it clearer still, and delimit the concerns more precisely. 'Feminism and Writing: Poetry . . . Drama . . .'; 'Feminism and Writing: Questions of Difference . . . of Race . . . of Class . . . of Sexuality'; 'Current Themes . . . Changing Themes'.

So, there we were in 1984 with a course entitled 'The Position of the Feminist Writer'. In the course itself we wanted to start discussing the way women and feminists were meshed together but, at some crucial point, veered away from each other. We wanted to explore what feminism had changed for women, as writers and as readers. We were interested in whether feminism had changed the kinds of topics it was now possible to write about, or just what was said. We focused on love, sex and spirituality. We looked at the way feminism challenged popular conceptions about what kind of people writers were, and looked at the writing of women whose work was no less important to them, and their readers, simply because they chose not to define themselves as 'writers' but as 'women who write', alongside the myriad other things they did with their lives. We also looked at women who clearly did see themselves as writers, and asked what sort of differences feminism was making to their lives. And, partly because the archetypal image of a woman reader is a woman with her head not in a book but in a magazine, we looked at the impact of feminism upon women's magazines, including a detailed look at *Spare Rib* and other feminist publishing initiatives.

Such wide-ranging themes and open-ended questions over a nine-week course were extremely ambitious and the outline we give here would easily work over, say, twenty or twenty-four weeks. Our intention was to stimulate students into further reading and thinking on their own. So, for example, we used short extracts from works in the hope that students would be sufficiently interested to read the whole book at a later date. For most students, this did happen, but obviously had it been possible for them to read an entire book prior to discussion or during the course itself, the complexity and depth of our discussions would have been enriched. It would also have been feasible to involve students in their own research or writing projects linked to the course. Our intention was to enable learning from discussion based on personal experience, and remembered, as well as recent, reading. Our role as tutors was to make connections, trigger off memory and guide students into contemplating and then discussing areas of experience that were hitherto isolated or unknown to them.

The course outline was as follows:

Week 1 Introductions
Discussion: What do we understand by feminism?
What has been our experience of and involvement with feminism?
Week 2 Feminist Criticism and Women in Literature
Week 3 *Spare Rib* – Our Magazine?
Week 4 Feminism and Women's Magazines
Week 5 Women's Spirituality
Week 6 Sex and Sexuality
Week 7 Poetry
Week 8 Writing the Future: women utopian/dystopian writers
Week 9 Success: women's movement stars

We gave this out with a two-part reading list at our first session: essential reading; and helpful reading, consisting of books we would refer to and provide extracts from. Carefully constructed reading lists are an important resource for students and it is worth spending time on them. Breaking down the essential and recommended reading is useful, as it prevents the list being off-putting to students with little time for reading and not much experience of using a library. A brief summary of the book's content will help students who are only just beginning to read studiously and systematically:

Reading List

Part 1

A Piece of the Night, Michèle Roberts (Women's Press)
The Visitation, Michèle Roberts (Women's Press)

Benefits, Zoë Fairbairns (Virago)
The Dispossessed, Ursula Le Guin (Granada)

Part 2

Hard Feelings, ed. Alison Fell (Women's Press)
Spare Rib Reader, ed. Marsha Rowe (Penguin)
Everyday Matters, ed. Sheba Collective (Sheba)
Love Your Enemy? Leeds Rev. Feminist Gp. (Onlywomen)
Sex and Love, ed. S. Cartledge and J. Ryan (Women's Press)
Walking on the Water, ed. J. Garcia and S. Maitland (Virago)
The World Split Open, ed. Louise Bernikow (Women's Press)

Having discussed the course outline, we began the discussion about feminism with a brainstorm around the words 'Woman' and 'Feminist'. This was rather forced: probably the group weren't relaxed enough at that early stage. A better way, early on in a group, or where members are very shy and quiet, is to ask each person to write down three, or five things that the word suggests to them. These are then gathered together and discussed, roughly along the lines of:

Is there a pattern. If so, what is it?
What isn't there?
Where do these associations come from?
Are there any other questions which follow from the list?

The lists, which were constructed one after another, were as follows:

Feminist – Woman, Women, Oppressed women, Dungarees, Short hair, Stereotyped women.
Woman – Venus, Bodies, Ourselves, Plump and ugly, Work, Ovaries, Children, Lifeboats (Women and children first).

We discussed these lists and then moved on to work in pairs through the following questions, which we reported back to the whole group:

1 Would you call yourself a feminist?
2 Would anybody else call you a feminist? If so, what would your reaction be?

3 Have you ever been involved in any feminist campaigns? If so, what and when? Can you remember how you first got involved?

4 If you haven't been involved in any feminist campaigns, was this a deliberate decision?

5 What were your reasons for coming to this course?

An alternative introduction at this stage would be to divide the group into twos or threes and give each a different, polemical, quotation about feminists and feminism and to discuss their reactions to it. A mixture of contemporary and historical extracts would be important in establishing that feminism isn't a late twentieth-century phenomenon, as would attention to the issues of race and class. Provocative writers about feminism include: Norman Mailer, Beatrix Campbell, Julie Burchill, Anna Livia, Germaine Greer, Wilmette Brown – not to mention copywriters in the *Sun*, *The Daily Telegraph* and *Daily Express*, high court judges, Conservative MPs and peers of the realm. Dictionary definitions, especially from *The Feminist Dictionary* and *The Wickedary*, can also shed an interesting light on attitudes.

The second session began with a short discussion about how to define women's writing and what was distinctive about women's writing that was also feminist. We then discussed, as a group, our response to the following questions:

1 Do you mostly read books by women?

2 Have you always?

3 Who publishes the books you usually buy or borrow?

4 Do you think of the books you read as being women's books, feminist books or just books?

The discussion established that most of us now mainly read books by women, although almost all our early reading had been male. There were often no women writers made available to us at school, except perhaps *Jane Eyre* in an abridged version. Our teenage reading, if we carried on that long, tended to be French or American male authors often with quite unpleasant attitudes towards women. We tended to look out for the distinctive presentation of Virago and Women's Press titles. The definition of 'women' which we preferred to 'feminist' for our books was as sharply distinguished from traditional, romantic women's writing as it was from feminist writing. We agreed that feminism was important for the writers and to some extent for us too, but we also felt uncomfortable with its suggestion of a cramped, moralistic view of the world.

We then gave students a nine-page handout which brought together extracts from a variety of academic sources. The handout was prefaced by Virginia Woolf's introduction to her essay, *A Room of One's Own*:

> The title women and fiction might mean, and you may have meant it to mean, women and what they are like; or it might mean women and the fiction that they write; or it might mean women and the fiction that is written about them; or it might mean that somehow all three are inextricably mixed together and you want me to consider them in that light.
>
> (Woolf 1945: 5)

The handout also contained substantial extracts from:
1 'Women's Language and Literature: A Problem in Women's Studies', by Kate McKluskie, from *Feminist Review* 14. The extract we chose illustrated the author's disagreement with Dale Spender's theory of a 'Man-Made' language, elaborated with reference to the writings of Adrienne Rich:

> how could men in a pre-linguistic state have communicated in order to conspire – but it provides a powerful image which seems to reflect the reality of women's experience.

and 2 'What Women's Literature?' by Minda Rae Amiran, in *College English*. In this piece the author establishes her credentials as a feminist since the 1950s and stresses that she supports the political struggle of feminists today. However, she is at great pains to detach that politics from the study of literature:

> the teaching of women's literature in English departments [is] a subversion of women's liberation. The whole point of leaving the doll's house, I would have thought, was to become a person among people.

and 3 'Are Women's Novels Feminist Novels?', by Rosalind Coward, in *Feminist Review* 5. Here the author argues that women-centred writing, far from having any special relationship with feminism, is equally characteristic of the popular romance, with its concentration on the consciousness of an individual heroine.

Struggling to define what, if anything, does mark a novel out as 'feminist', she settles for their confessional, quasi-autobiographical style of narration:

> the voice of the central protagonist, if not presenting itself directly as the author's voice, frequently offers itself as 'representative' of women in general, firstly claiming sexual experiences as a vital terrain of all women's experience, sometimes also making generalities as to the oppressive nature of that experience.

and 4 'Towards a Feminist Poetics', by Elaine Showalter, in *The New Feminist . . . Criticism*, which gives a brief guide to the varieties of feminist criticism which have developed:

> the feminist critique is essentially political and polemical, with theoretical affiliations to Marxist sociology and aesthetics; gynocritics is more self-contained and experimental, with connections to other modes of new feminist research. . . .
> It can guide authors who are writing literary works from a new feminist perspective, as well as those critics who are analyzing existing literature.

and 5 'Feminists, Feminism and Writing', by Ellen Cronan Rose, in *Women and Writing Newsletter* 3. This is a brief report on research work carried out in the summer of 1979. On a visiting lectureship from the USA, Ellen had been interested by the sudden blossoming of feminist writing and theatre. She spoke to a wide cross-section of feminist writers:

> I began with one absolutely basic question (other issues arose in the course of the interview): what criteria would you use to identify and define 'feminist literature'? . . . I found myself asking with increasing frequency, the question: 'To what degree does your feminism liberate or constrain you as a writer?'

This handout introduced questions which would inform the rest of the course, acting as a guide as well as providing an overview of current thinking about feminist criticism. To summarise, they were:

1 What is women's relation to language?

2 Is feminist or women's literature a valid way to approach literature?
3 Is women's writing the same as feminist writing?
4 What differences do the terms 'women' and 'feminist' indicate?
5 How does feminist criticism talk about women's writing?
6 What do feminist writers think about feminist writing?

We moved, in the third week, from these quite difficult theoretical issues to the more accessible area of women's magazines. This gave students an opportunity to read ahead, as the novels we had wanted to concentrate on were coming up in weeks five and eight. Magazines were chosen as a way in for other reasons, too. Their size makes it easy to compare a range of them during one session, and allows students to take control of the materials, and to make their own investigations. It is also a topic which, unlike some of the later ones, we could be fairly confident everyone knew something about: even if they didn't read a magazine regularly themselves, they would see one when they went to the dentist or doctor, or perhaps their mother read one. Also, beginning with *Spare Rib* was an unthreatening way to introduce the preoccupations of contemporary feminism to those women who were unfamiliar with them.

We began this session by taking the class through a set of orientating questions. This can be a very useful way into any class discussion, but – as with any other teaching technique – if used for every session it will begin to pall. We asked students to think about and answer the following questions, based just on their existing knowledge of *Spare Rib*:

1 Who is *Spare Rib* aimed at?
2 Who is it written by?
3 Is it representative of all women?
4 Is *Spare Rib* a feminist magazine?
5 Who controls it/how is it controlled?
6 What, if anything, do you read it for?

This started a discussion about the aims of the magazine and how far it succeeded in them, as well as helping us establish who was familiar with the magazine and who wasn't.

We used that basic framework of questions to introduce the magazine's history. This presentation was supplemented with extracts from letters pages over the years and actual copies of the magazine from 1972 onwards. We also had on display the various anthologies from *Spare Rib* which have been produced – *Hard Feelings* and *Spare Rib: A Reader*.

In preparation for this session, we had researched the changing nature of the magazine since its publication in July 1972. The questions we asked were:

1 What are the aims of the magazine? What does it claim to represent?
2 How is the magazine run?
3 Who does it see as its audience?
4 Does it have a class/race/sex bias?
5 What sort of advertisement does it have?
6 How much space is given to:
   fiction
   autobiographical writing
   poetry
   book reviews/articles about writers
   news
   features/polemic
   advice/d.i.y./information?
7 How much of the writing is by professional journalists/non-professional writers?
8 What do the letters tend to be about?
9 How much writing is there about: Black women, older women, young women, Irish women, lesbians, men, children, working-class women?

We broke this information down into tables and graphs and produced a sample breakdown for each year, following this model:

1972: Issue 1 June 17p
Edited: Marsha Rowe and Rosie Boycott

> We have tried to create a magazine that is fluid enough to publish work by contributors who have not written before as well as by women and men who are successful journalists and writers. We are waiting with bated breath for your reactions.

Concerns: Children: playgroups, childbirth, books and TV reviewed by kids; Abortion; Women's Aid; Work: Trade Unions, Fashion, Clerical; International News; Prostitution; Single Women;

Men; Health; the Law and your Rights; Heroin Addiction; Women's History.

There were also articles on: skin and hair care, fashion, d.i.y., recipes and knitting.

Letters: some from men, most from heterosexual, married women.

Writers were mostly professional, e.g. Angela Phillips, Sheila Rowbotham, Germaine Greer, Patricia Hewitt, Anna Raeburn, Mary Stott.

1973: Issue 17 November 20p

Edited: Marsha Rowe and Rosie Boycott

Concerns: Bigamy; Women in China; Poetry; Sculpture; Environment; Tax Credits; Battered Women; Childcare; Sex – Anna Raeburn's Agony Column; Asian Women; Racism

Letters: all from women, about: contraception; stigma of illegitimacy; complaining about tone of male correspondents; commenting on women's liberation as a reversal of male/female domination, not its eradication.

We also talked about, and brought in examples of, the range of feminist and women's liberation movement publishing: *Women's Report*; *Women's Voice*; *Shrew*; *Red Rag*; *Outwrite*; *Sappho;* *Scarlet Woman*; *Spinster*; *WIRES*; *Shocking Pink*; *Feminist Review*, as well as copies of local women's papers and newsletters. We talked about the emphasis on print and communication, the pull between the need to communicate within a movement of women and the desire to propagandise beyond it.

There was a mixed response to *Spare Rib*, particularly from those who had been regular readers. There was a sense of duty about reading it for some women, although we could identify a time when it had been urgent and important reading for us. These times did not coincide and therefore were probably more to do with the process of our own politicisation than with the magazine. At the time, deep and protracted struggles about racism and imperialism were going on within the collective which produced the magazine, and these debates and arguments were conducted in its pages. While everyone agreed that the issues raised were of major importance, there was also a sense that in buying *Spare Rib* at that time you were eavesdropping on partial, almost private quarrels. There was also a consensus that

11

the magazine had narrowed its concerns, from an attempt, however misguided, to appeal to all women, in order to cater for politically active women, although there was very little coverage, except in news shorts, of party politics or socialist organising. There is perhaps a tendency for feminists to be more critical of the magazine's shortcomings and to be aware of the subtleties of its ideological bias. Women encountering the magazine for the first time will generally find it an exciting read, and appreciate the different perspective and information it provides.

In the following week, we turned our attention to the traditional women's magazine sector. This is an area of study that has attracted a lot of research and writing. Our focus was the impact that feminism has had on these magazines' style and coverage. In 1984, that was far less marked than it is today, where a whole swatch of new magazines – *Best*, *Elle*, *Marie Claire* – for young and older women alike, cater directly to the independent, working woman. There are a number of lines of enquiry for students, especially in looking at images of women, which they can do independently.

We began with a short talk about the history and development of women's magazines, drawing on the work of Cynthia White, Judith Williamson and Janice Winship. Although there were very marked differences between magazines at any given period, which is partly a class distinction, but also to do with which dominant version of femininity they were promoting, it was also possible to characterise differences between periods. So, for example, the 1950s had been very concentrated on 'the home', and consumer durables were everywhere in evidence. By the 1960s, the emphasis had changed to youth and fashion, and by the 1970s it was changing again, to a version of independence for women that did not undermine, although it transformed, traditional femininity. In the 1980s that image changes again, becoming highly sexualised and fetishistically passive. Some of the most interesting changes in women's magazine publishing concern the weeklies rather than the more upmarket magazines which cater for their imagined independent readers. *Woman* and *Woman's Own* now regularly cover topics such as rape, returning to work, sex surveys, domestic violence, environmental issues, etc., that five or ten years ago would have been featured in *Spare Rib*, and would have been considered extreme.

We discussed the following questions:

1 How and why do you think women read magazines?
2 Have you ever regularly read a magazine?
 If so, what influenced you to choose it?
 Were you satisfied with it?
 Did you change or stop?
3 If not, do you ever read magazines, and if so, when and where?

We brought in a selection of current magazines and, together, drew up a checklist of ways to assess feminism's impact. The list centred upon things like:

What sort of advertising does it carry: range of products and services, proportion of ads to features, classified or full-colour images? What are the images? Does the look of the magazine come from its advertising or its features?
What assumptions do the articles make about how a woman spends her time and the views she holds?
What leisure interests does the magazine assume you have?
Does it assume you have leisure? Is reading it work or leisure?
How does it handle sex?
What sort of problem page does it have?
What sort of morality and values inform the answers?
What kind of issues are featured?
What sort of women appear in the magazine: age, race, active/passive, alone, or with the family or other women?
What sort of women appear in the ads: age, race, whole or in parts?
Who is writing for the magazine?
How much of the magazine is devoted to the household and children?
How do the editors see their typical woman reader?
What is omitted?

We were all struck by how much the magazines featured royalty, film stars and celebrities. Women like the magazine's readers were almost entirely absent, so the magazine provided fantasy and gossip rather than guidance about everyday life and problems or role models. There was quite a heated debate about what the magazines should offer. One side of the argument saw them as trivialising the readers' own lives and inculcating an unhealthy attitude of envy and admiration for the very wealthy. The other side thought women knew the reality of their own lives far too well and were entitled to be taken out of themselves if they wanted to be. Although our group did not pursue it at the time, there was an interesting discussion about the way the news media, especially TV, represents women and women's issues.

Spirituality, the subject of our fifth session, was included for a number of reasons. We wanted to approach feminism as a source of both public and private change. The timely publication of *Walking on the Water*, a collection of writing about women's spirituality, allowed considerable debate about the volume; an added bonus was the inclusion in *Walking* of a lengthy piece by Michèle Roberts, a writer we had wanted to discuss in our session. Also, spirituality reflected our own particular concerns and interests. We had not been involved in organised religion since our early teens, but we shared a fascination with its cultural offshoots: churches, especially Catholic ones; painting and music; as well as a developed appreciation of ritual. We were also intrigued by the female saints and martyrs, by nuns and by contemplative solitude.

Looking back, it seems astonishing to have viewed spirituality through such a Eurocentric frame. The meshing of spirituality with political resistance and change throughout the Black communities of the past and present is in itself an oversight of massive proportion. Linked to the spirituality informing the writing of Toni Morrison, Alice Walker and Toni Cade Bambara, it underlines how partial was our understanding of the power for women that spirituality represents.

We began the session by discussing in pairs what our religious background had been and what we felt about it now. That led us into a discussion about spirituality: what it was; whether there was, or needed to be, a women's spirituality; how far spirituality depended upon religion; how far creativity of any kind depended upon a spiritual awareness. We introduced this by offering our own understanding of spirituality. We began with spirituality's concern with the spirit and the soul as opposed to the body and matter. We saw it as the spaces in between the everyday struggle for existence, the place where we come to a sense of ourselves. Identity does not come just from a function or a position. What does it mean, we asked, to say, 'I am a this or a that, a teacher, feminist, woman, mother. Where is the sense of wholeness in ourselves? Who are we when we're alone?'

We then discussed the various ways in which that sense of wholeness is achieved or struggled for. Religion is the most obvious place to look, but for those of us in this group, religion had either always been, or rapidly become, hollow and hypocritical. Some people had turned, usually briefly, from religion to the fringe activities of the Tarot, I Ching or astrology as a way of seeing purpose and meaning in their lives, or to the religions of the East, such as Buddhism, or to various gurus. The way in which love and friendship give that same sense of meaning and wholeness was talked about at some length. There was disagreement about whether it was damaging or not. We were all conscious of the dangers for women in negating their own selves under the false lure of romance, but at the same time we recognised how powerful and illuminating of our lives and selves certain friendships were. The detaching of that love from sexual involvement was a key distinction made here.

Creativity, whether as books, art or music, seemed to be one of the most common ways the spiritual world was kept alive for us. It could be as participants, creators or consumers. There were parallels between the nature of creativity and the nature of spirituality, in their demands for withdrawal from the workaday world. The natural world was a source of contemplation and satisfaction, as were certain forms of physical activity, especially swimming and walking alone.

We then looked in detail at the work of Michèle Roberts. We had asked students to read *A Piece of the Night* and *The Visitation* and had handed out copies of 'The Woman Who Wanted to Be a Hero', her contribution to *Walking on the Water*. We chose Roberts because she is a writer clearly concerned with spirituality who has used her religious background for much of her most potent imagery. Her writing also draws on her experiences in a much wider sense, focusing on her relationship with her mother and grandmother, the time she spent in Thailand and so on. She is also very committed to feminism and identifies herself first and foremost as a feminist writer.

A Piece of the Night

> Over the next four years, I began to reel in my catch, exploring with a lot of fear, the connections I found I made between Catholicism, sexuality, repression, mother and daughter.
>
> (Roberts in Garcia and Maitland 1983: 50)

The novel is made up of many layers passing backwards and forwards in time. Julie Fanchot is visiting her mother who is ill in France, and leaves her daughter, Bertha, in the women's house in South London she shares with three other women and one other child. The house is owned by, and now under threat from, Julie's ex-husband Ben. Julie attended a convent school with Jenny, who becomes her lover. This love links back to the past, to Amy who travelled in South-East Asia with Harriet, Ben's great, great aunt. When Harriet marries, Amy joins the Church and becomes Sister Veronica. It is her diary, an account of her travels and love for Harriet, which Julie takes with her when she leaves the marital home. Julie was a student at Oxford, a time which she spent in a state of terrible division and conflict. Eventually she goes mad. Passive and malleable, she marries Ben, a lecturer, when she discovers she is pregnant, and becomes submissive to his whims and manipulations.

The conflict at the heart of the novel is based on the Catholic view of womanhood, crudely expressed as the 'Virgin or the Whore', and women's aspiration to be the Virgin while constantly seeing themselves, and being seen, as the Whore. The book opens with the death of Sister Veronica, the final consummation at which the Bride of Christ joins her lover. It ends with Julie in conflict with Ben: he wishes to sell the house now they are divorced; she has finally come to believe in women's capacity to support and love each other. In between, the stories of Julie, her mother (who was seduced and pregnant when married), Amy/Sister Veronica and Harriet, and Jenny reflect the nature of women's position:

> If I cannot be a saint, so perfect that I need never suffer or know the pain of loss, then I will be the Devil . . . I am the witch whom you call your crazy daughter.
>
> (Roberts 1978: 108)

But this conflict, bitter and painfully real as it is, is an imposed conflict. Imposed by the church, and by men, who push onto women all the baggage of being Other: the dangerous, bestial parts of nature.

> I cause storms and migraines, I turn milk sour, I am both the ruined harvest and the shameful blood that sickens cattle.
>
> (Roberts 1978: 108)

16

The conflict Julie struggles with throughout the book is her own perception of womanhood – she is trying, simply, to find who she is. One way is through affirmation of her womanhood through sleeping with a man:

> to see, through his hitherto unknown and unmet sexual eyes, the self she essentially is at the same time as the self she may become . . . she does not know which to trust.
>
> (Roberts 1978: 67)

There is also Jenny, her woman lover, who offers possibilities infinitely more dangerous than this;

> The terror of positively establishing a whole self, or of discovering that there is no such simple entity, the fear of giving up the rules on how to see and discover her self.
>
> (Roberts 1978: 67)

Religion permeates the novel, providing its imagery and a psychic mesh from which Julie must free her self, her memory and future. It also works into the structure of the novel, where events from the religious calendar provide starting-points for circles and waves of memory, for connections and contrasts between Julie and other women. For example, the Feast of the Assumption occurs when Julie is in France and, as is the tradition, a celebratory lunch is cooked which Julie insists on preparing, but has to hand over to Suzette Cally, who gave up her job to return and nurse her own mother. This section, framed by the meal and the feast day, dwells on food. Julie remembers the food in England, how it was a source of interest to her but barely noticed by the English undergraduates, oblivious of the women working to put it on their plates and clear away again. There is the convent, with its strictures on food, and its conceit of food as an aid to contemplate the Lord's sacrifice.

> We restrain ourselves from eating as much as we wish, from taking pleasure in food, lest we forget the heavenly food of His body and blood He offers us each Mass.
>
> (Roberts 1978: 136)

Then, in her final memories of the baby's demands for food she turns the struggles between duty, love and hunger into an image of the unfulfilled hunger of women.

Michèle Roberts' second novel, *The Visitation*, was published five years later. She says of it:

17

I was surprised . . . to find myself writing a novel so passion-
ately concerned with the Creation, the Fall, the meaning of
original sin, the symbolism of the Garden of Eden, Eve as the
woman whose intellectual and sexual curiosity (I discovered
that these were intertwined) is named by patriarchy as bad.

(Roberts in Garcia and Maitland 1983: 61)

The Visitation is another multi-layered book. It is Helen's story, following her through childhood, with her twin, Felix; adolescence,
at university, with their friend Beth; the time she spent living in
Thailand with a lover and her return to England where she tries to
be a writer. The plot tracks her relationships with men (Stephen,
George and Robert) and with women (Beth, her mother and
grandmother). The novel is divided into two parts: 'Genesis' and
'The Visitation', and there are four visits from Beth which reflect
the seasons. The themes of the novel revolve around fulfilment
and from where, or from whom, it derives. Helen's search for
wholeness ultimately involves a synthesis of the masculine and
feminine within herself, which she traces back to Felix, and the
dislocations between them which began in childhood.

The Visitation has a complex story-line, weaving together Helen's
current relationships into a biblical and a mythic past. Alongside the
imagery of the Blessed Virgin Mary are other virgins, Artemis, or
Diana the hunter; and the incest taboo is explored, and pulled into
Helen's search for wholeness and synthesis:

She needs to embrace all these parts of herself if she is to live
without being maimed. Here are the twins after all; not, as
she once thought, bright separate meteors flashing across the
sky; not, as she once thought, warring archetypes exhausting
her energy. The twins lodge simply, deep inside her, as images
of different parts of herself, as needs for different sorts of
activity.

(Roberts 1983: 175)

The relationship between women friends is a major theme. When
Beth joins the Communist Party, a rift develops in her friendship
with Helen. Debates stemming from their ideas about belief and
spirituality continue throughout the novel, even after they have
re-established their friendship. It is Helen who makes the initial
move towards Beth. When Beth becomes pregnant, Helen at first
feels jealous and unhappy, excluded not just from Beth's friendship

but also from a sense of wholeness that motherhood offers. Beth's friendship is too important to risk again, however, because Beth believes in Helen as a writer whereas none of the men do. Beth's child starts to close the circle, back to her own child self, her one-ness with nature and the destruction of that by society's insistence on specific gender roles, and the taboos which it sets up around sex. And these destructive social patterns are seen as approved by and shored up by Christianity.

Michèle Roberts illustrates the feminist struggles with, and, at times, complete break with, the Christian traditions of the past. Traditional Christianity demarcated passive spirituality as the province of women, as well as allocating to women a considerable servicing role for men. Women have, of course, always been perfectly acceptable candidates for martyrdom, especially if virgins. Some of the most spectacular, and sadistic, martyrdoms involve women.

What women haven't had is any significant place in the hierarchy of church authority, and most religions have at their heart an ambivalence about women, expressed in sexual terms. Women have evolved certain forms of spiritual guidance and wisdom outside traditional religions: as healers, wise women and in the passage of information between mothers and daughters, but this has been feared and ridiculed by men, when not ignored by them. Women, too, are sometimes suspicious of these female figures, used as we are to see only in men the really powerful and useful kinds of knowledge.

Teaching about spirituality now, we would look more closely at the traditions of Black women's involvement with Christian religion and spirituality, as well as at religious traditions other than the Judaeo-Christian. The contemporary debates about the ordination of women could figure more prominently, and good use could be made of the work Elaine Hobby has done into the relationship, in the seventeenth century, between women, writing and religion. Sara Maitland's account of more contemporary views and positions in *A Map of the New Country*, 1982, would also be useful.

We considered spirituality as just one dimension of feminist concern and writing, but it would certainly bear extension into a course of its own. In doing that, proper attention could be given to the historical dimension of women and spirituality, as it could to the cross-racial and cross-cultural implications. The divergence and convergence between an interest in spirituality and psychotherapy, and their respective influence on women's writing, could also be explored in detail.

Organised religion had a lot to say about sexuality, as does the women's liberation movement, and so we turned next to consider questions of sex and sexuality. We began with quite a simple question that in fact generated a wide-ranging and quite fascinating discussion about the formation of our sexual identities and role models; where we got our sexual information from; how we felt about reading about sex; the different ways in which men and women wrote about sexual behaviours and feelings. The question was:

What books have expressed, or had an effect upon, your sexuality?

As this discussion died away, we gave a prepared talk which summarised the thinking, organising and writing about sex and sexuality from within the women's liberation movement.

Briefly, we located the rise of contemporary feminism as a result of reaction to male dominance of the Left and of the sexual libertarianism that flourished in the 1960s and 1970s. Identifying consciousness-raising as a forum to discuss sex, we charted the shift away from an assumption that sexuality meant heterosexuality to the organising around lesbianism as a political issue which culminated in the Sixth Demand of the women's liberation movement, adopted at the 1974 Edinburgh conference. The belief that there was such a thing as feminist sexual politics, indeed the elision of feminism into sexual politics, prevailed generally within the movement. We finally considered how heterosexual women tended increasingly towards silence about their sexual hopes, fears and practice. Lesbians began to dominate the discussions about sexuality at a personal level, and the public political campaigns, about pornography, about sexual violence against women, added to the silencing, and often to the guilt, of heterosexual women.

We looked, too, at how women saw sex outside the women's liberation movement. At the time, we had access only to the surveys carried out by magazines such as *Company* and *Cosmopolitan*. Nowadays, *Women and Love* by Shere Hite would give a far more systematic insight into the subject. The collections of writing by women about sex, whether theoretical and polemical or fictional, would also be good sources: *Deep Down: New Sensual Writing by Women*, ed. Laura Chester; *Serious Pleasure*, ed. Sheba Collective;

Pleasure and Danger, ed. C. Vance. We found, in *Cosmopolitan* of
February 1979, an article listing the questions most asked about
sex. They included queries about the value of aphrodisiacs, anxiety
about how normal or not their genitals were; oral sex and anal sex;
anxiety about orgasm; venereal disease.

Moving on to consider creative writers in particular, we saw
how problems of language limit what women can or will say. It
has become increasingly difficult to separate out writing about sex
– in any but the most clinical versions – from pornography or a
language associated with men, not women. Sex, in the women's
liberation movement, also seemed to attract an alarming set of
proscriptions: correct and incorrect practice and an underlying
assumption that sexual compatibility and bliss come with ideological compatibility. Penetration became an issue, within heterosexual
and lesbian relationships. Questions of monogamy and promiscu-
ity, jealousy and romantic love also came in for lengthy debate.

We looked at the way Kate Millett and Gillian Hanscombe dealt
with these themes and at the importance of books such as *Shedding*,
The Shame is Over and *Flying*. We suggested that some women
responded deeply to these books because they found expression
of their own feelings and experiences in the repetitive masochistic
pattern of women's sexual experience. This is something which
seems inevitable once women internalise, as everything in society
urges them to, a sense of self-objectification within sexual relationships, whether their partners are men or other women. We
also looked at how some writers seemed to make a separation
between what could be worked out with a particular man individually and the common experiences women have of a heterosexist,
male-dominated world.

We referred women to those writers who we felt had attempted
to consider the potential of a feminist sexual practice. *Woman on
the Edge of Time* by Marge Piercy and *Between Friends* by Gillian
Hanscombe, in particular, seemed to cover the range of issues
involved. Although very different as novels (one jumps off from
twentieth-century North American poverty into a futuristic world,
the other is set in the contemporary world, and is a series of letters
between four women who are facing very different sorts of issues
about sexuality, motherhood, love and friendship), they share the
ability to confront the question of power in sexual relationships.

We used this concern with power as a way into the article 'Sensual
Uncertainty or Why the Clitoris is Not Enough' by Lynne Segal

in the collection *Sex and Love: New Thoughts on Old Contradictions.* We also considered, in the light of the essay, the idea of a natural, unique female sexuality that lay somehow unbesmirched under the dross of patriarchal assumption and exploitation, waiting to be rediscovered and redirected for ourselves. This led on to discussion of lesbian sexuality, which is seen by many women, lesbian or not, as the model for that sexuality. Lesbianism sometimes becomes the vanguard of feminism, which implies that lesbians don't, or shouldn't have, any kind of sexual difficulties at all. This is far from being the case. What lesbians often have is a more equal possibility of working out their sexual problems, but this is not automatic, nor are they always possible to resolve. This position is stated very clearly in Wendy Clarke's essay 'The Dyke, the Feminist and the Devil' in *Feminist Review* 11, 1982.

We ended our talk with two more questions:

What would you see as positive descriptions of sex for women?
Why do we write about, or read about, sex?

We then discussed four poems, copies of which had been given out the previous week, along with the Lynne Segal article. These were:

'Against Coupling' by Fleur Adcock, from *The Penguin Book of Contemporary Verse* (about masturbation)
'Coming Out Celibate' by Astra, from *One Foot on the Mountain* (about celibacy)
'In Confidence' by Alison Fell, from *Smile, Smile, Smile, Smile* (about orgasms)
'Now as I Begin to Age' by Sheila Shulman, from *One Foot on the Mountain* (about lesbianism)

The decision to give out examples of poetry was partly because there was a lot of reading already (the long article), and we were referring to novels in the introductory talk which we hoped women would read fairly soon. It also provided a way into the following week's session on poetry, by indicating how useful poetry had been to feminists wanting to explore and communicate ideas about personal and immediate issues that seemed, at the same time, to be of wider, more social importance.

By looking at feminism and poetry we actually wanted to focus less on the content of the work and its challenge to literary convention, although these are fruitful and exciting areas to pursue, but more on poetry as an example of the way feminism had the potential to open up channels of communication and access to print.

By way of introducing the session, we summarised the impact feminism has had on creativity, noting that there was a great deal of interest in reclaiming work from the past, that theatre had been more amenable to feminism than had TV, and that poetry was everywhere. This struck us as odd, given that poetry is the most privileged of the literary forms, the most exclusive. We did a quick straw poll around the room and elicited from some women a sense of poetry as boring, difficult and not something they would often choose to read. These women, as well as the rest of the class, had found the poems we gave out the previous week interesting and enjoyable and were surprised in some ways to have to think of them as poetry. Women who did read poetry tended not to read in the classic tradition, but rather to read the anthologised work of contemporary women, some of whom were not professional writers or, as with the groups that produced *Licking the Bed Clean, Cutlasses and Earrings*, and *Smile, Smile, Smile, Smile*, did not confine their interest in writing to one form. Some women, too, had read the poets of the Mersey Sound and other popular poets of the late 1960s and 1970s.

We then worked our way through a handout which had been given, with a brief introduction, the week before. It contained:

1 The whole of the introduction by Louise Bernikow to *The World Split Open*
2 An extract from the preface to *The Penguin Book of Women Poets* by Carol Cosman, Joan Keefe and Kathleen Weaver
3 An extract from the introduction to *Hard Feelings*, a collection of writings from *Spare Rib*, edited by Alison Fell
4 An extract from the article 'Feminism and the Poetic Tradition' by Janet Montefiore in *Feminist Review* 13

Each extract was intended to help us to focus on particular questions. Louise Bernikow discussed the survival of women poets and the evaluation of their writing, and introduced the idea of traditions of women's writing, and the importance of tradition to their writing. She also stressed content as much as form as a subject of study and enquiry. There was a suggestion in her work that we should read women's poetry as:

Historical documentation in itself;
In relation to socio-economic history;
As texts for the study of consciousness in poetry.

We concluded by discussing her views on what women can write about – she asserts that women can write about love, always a less exalted topic when women write about it than when men do, and religion:

> The gap between what interests women and what interests men has locked women poets into a paralyzing contradiction from which some have emerged and to which others have succumbed. Women's lives bore men. The reality of those lives, especially the embarrassing subject of women's bodies, frightens men. Male approval, the condition of a poet's survival, is withheld when a woman shapes her poetry from the very material that contradicts and threatens male reality.
>
> (Bernikow 1979: 7)

The preface from the introduction to *The Penguin Book of Women Poets* was included by way of a contrast to *The World Split Open*. Despite its very pertinent and interesting reflections about the point at which women poets became poetesses, with all the negative connotations that term entails, the collection raises some problems. It includes work in translation from a wide range of countries through a historical spectrum ranging from 1567 BC to the present day. There is, inevitably, very little from each poet and it is an impossible task to provide contexts for the poets, whether biographical, historical or literary. It is compiled in a spirit of redressing the balance and encouraging a wider appreciation of women's poetry but it doesn't, as Louise Bernikow does so well, account for the opposition to women as poets and the lack of interest in their work.

Alison Fell, herself a poet and former fiction editor for *Spare Rib*, compiled an anthology of work published in the magazine during its first seven years. We looked at an extract from her introduction to it. The kinds of issues it raised for discussion included whether she was right in her contention that *Spare Rib* was the natural home for the creative work produced by the women's liberation movement. In the light of *Spare Rib*'s policy, in force now for a number of years, not to accept unsolicited poetry and fiction, this particular debate is closed. However, the more general point about whether you write for your peers or direct your work outwards, either to succeed financially or to communicate your views, is still a live one. We also found much to stimulate our discussion in her account of how the criteria for selecting material had changed as an increasing number of women started to write and send in their work.

Our final extract, from Janet Montefiore's article in *Feminist Review*, was a more difficult, academic piece of writing and in order to ease that shift in style, we selected a piece where she compares Lucy Boston's 'Hybrid Perpetual' with Alison Fell's 'Girl's Gifts', two poems which make very different uses of flower imagery. In Boston's poem, a sexual message is to the fore, and a sexuality is implied which depends for its opening on a masculinised sun. In Fell's, a child makes a gift of a little flower basket for her grandmother, watched by her mother, thus turning the flower away from its sexual associations and focusing us towards a social world of women, one that protects and nurtures and in which the child is free to give, and wants to give, her gifts. The whole question of flower imagery is an interesting one and could be supplemented by visual images – Georgia O'Keefe's painting comes immediately to mind. Janet Montefiore's article was work in progress for *Feminism and Poetry*, published by Pandora in 1987.

Montefiore argues against the position outlined by Bernikow and Fell. The idea of a woman's tradition is, she says, so all-encompassing as to become meaningless. The question of the relationship between women and feminism comes up again, but also the sense that some differences between women are so great that it is positively unhelpful to try and seek a common denominator. She does feel, however, that it is valuable to try to isolate the specifically feminist nature of poems and looks for it in structure as well as in content. In class, we appreciated the opportunity to see some very detailed comparative analyses of poetry, which sparked off an interesting discussion about whether we would analyse poems in that way and what was gained from such close attention.

We also discussed the ways in which groups of women had been able not just to support each other as writers but also to publish their work. The range varied enormously, from heavy duty paperbacks receiving wide circulation, like *Smile, Smile, Smile, Smile*, to duplicated collections, mostly sold locally to friends and acquaintances of the women involved in the writing group. 'Don't Come Looking Here', a collection from women in Birmingham;

'Shush, Mum's Writing' from Bristol and 'Gyn/erate', which arose from a summer school organised by the WEA in Staffordshire, were of interest. We referred students to Lucy Whitman's article on 'Community Publishing' in *Spare Rib* 115, February 1982, and drew on our own experience as workers at Centerprise, one of the leading community publishers. Some women in the community publishing movement were deeply suspicious of the word 'feminism'. Their identity was very firmly as working-class, and they perceived the women's liberation movement as removed from and uninterested in their experiences of life.

Within the feminist movement, the access afforded by offset printing tended to be used in one of two ways. Magazines or newspapers would be produced which carried a range of articles and features, often including poetry or fiction. These catered either for a particular locality, such as 'Cleveland Women's Newsletter', 'Birmingham Women's Paper', or for a particular interest or campaign group, such as Feminists Against Sexual Terrorism, Christian Feminists. Rather than have a writing group which occasionally published a collection of its work, as happened in the working-class-based community publishing movement, feminists tended to set up presses: so, a number of women's presses developed, such as Straumullion, Onlywomen, Sheba, I.F.I, Jezebel and Arlen House, as well as the 'market leaders' of Virago and the Women's Press. And a tendency arose to form feminist imprints within the larger publishing houses, for example, Pandora. But no feminist poetry press was set up, despite the proliferation of small press poetry publishers in Britain during the 1960s and 1970s.

It seemed that feminist energy was limited to the writing-workshop side of poetry: when it came to publication, women were left to fend for themselves to a large extent. The journal *Writing Women*, produced in Newcastle since the early 1980s, is now the sole forum for women which encourages new writers. Attempts to establish magazines, such as *Women's Review* and *Women Live*, have run into financial difficulties associated with low circulation. The established feminist presses don't publish much poetry, and publish even less by up-and-coming writers. The most successful poetry publications from the women's presses are works by well-known women such as Maya Angelou or Alice Walker, or anthologies like *In the Pink* and *The Raving Beauties*, which rely to some extent on the performance of the work by both established and new writers, for their success. Virago launched a poetry list in 1984 with four collections by individual women, none of whom could be considered new writers. While this is par for the course when it comes to poetry publishing, there does seem to be a dearth of opportunities for up-and-coming feminist poets to develop and publish their writing in comparison with prose writers or playwrights.

Our eighth session looked at women writing about the future, not as polemic, but through fiction in utopian or dystopian writing. We concentrated on Zoë Fairbairns' novel *Benefits*, which we put into a context of women's relationship to science fiction and utopian writing. As we taught the course in 1984, our immediate reference point was George Orwell's novel *Nineteen Eighty-Four*, but we also talked about other male writing in that genre, including Anthony Burgess's *Clockwork Orange*. We also considered the ways in which women used the concepts of utopia and dystopia. Much of women's utopian writing has a religious theme and is problematic for feminists for that reason. *Eve and the New Jerusalem* (Virago 1983), Barbara Taylor's impressive study of women's contribution to the nineteenth-century movements for utopian socialism, is undoubtedly relevant to these concerns.

We talked about Charlotte Perkins Gilman's *Herland*, a nineteenth-century utopia which was reissued by the Women's Press in 1979 and then again as part of their science fiction list. We discussed the work of Ursula Le Guin and Doris Lessing, noting how both writers have a more pessimistic than optimistic view of the future. This linked in well with *Benefits*, which presents a very bleak view of a future world and raises thorny questions about feminist demands for recognition and payment for domestic work and childrearing.

This is in very marked contrast to the work subsequently produced by the Women's Press for their science fiction list, which tends towards the optimistic, whether through humour or simply an imagined better world. When we taught this course, the Women's Press were just starting to commission that list. Nowadays, the frame of reference for this session would need to be much wider as their impressive list has brought together new and exciting writers in the genre, such as Jane Palmer and Josephine Saxron as well as introducing American writers such as Joanna Russ and Suzette Haden Elgin to new audiences. Their anthology, *Despatches from the Frontiers of the Female Mind* and Sarah Lefanu's critical study, *In the Chinks of the World Machine* again provide material for a whole course.

We welcomed the opportunity, however, to focus in detail on a single book, especially one which pulled together many of the themes of the earlier sessions. *Benefits* highlights the preoccupations of feminism's earliest days, it has a range of themes connected with sexuality and sexual relations, it touches on spirituality, makes the political issues about separatism dynamic to the plot and discusses motherhood and mothering at some length, issues which already had informed much feminist thinking and writing. In addition, it is written by one of the members of the first feminist writing and publishing group, which produced *Tales I Tell my Mother* in 1978 with an introduction by her setting out some of their collective agreements and disagreements about the nature of feminism and writing.

The action of *Benefits* takes place in three widely-spaced years: 1976, 1984, 2001, and it passes smoothly from one year to another. We begin with The Women, a separatist feminist group squatting in an empty tower block. The political themes of the novel centre on women's fertility: the right to choose, the attempt by men to impose control, the implications for women of being primary carers of children, whether singly or collectively. There is a tension about taking, or demanding, wages for housework, about accepting their benefit.

It doesn't look too good in 1976, sweltering in a heatwave, arguing with male trade unionists about child benefit and income tax, but by 1984 those arguments seem a luxury. The Family Party exercises its control and the country is gripped by a moral panic about 'suitable' women opting out of maternity, and 'unsuitable' women who are still producing children. The welfare state is finally dismantled and in its place comes benefit, motherhood as national service, which brings in its wake the surveillance, and rehabilitation, of women who refuse, or are 'bad' at motherhood.

By 2001 Planned Population is the currency of international trade and economic agreements, but it all starts to go disastrously wrong. Out of this, a political force is generated in women who were formerly opposed to each other and, working together, they create pressure points on the reinstated social democratic party.

Unlike most novels of ideas, *Benefits* develops its women characters in some depth. It is always the story of an issue, but against the historical changes of the novel, the question of how Marsha and Lynne relate to each other, their lovers, children, sisters in the women's liberation movement, is played out in all its complexity.

Benefits sustains, despite its sharper focus on the characters Marsha and Lynne, a sense of feminism as a concern of women *en masse*; it captures the claustrophobic comfort and excitement of large groups of women working, living, arguing, being together. Sisterhood and collectivity was one of the first principles of the women's liberation movement. It set itself against competitive individualism and located self-development and fulfilment firmly in the context of the group and the collective. How then did the women's liberation movement, and how did we, deal with success and stars? Was it just the media's need to pick off individual women? Was it simply careerism? How do we evaluate and criticise our movement's writing? How is it received by the literary establishment? Does success bring with it any special responsibility for feminists? These questions shaped our final session.

Quite by chance Hilary Bailey, in her review of the week's new fiction, provided us with a starting-point for discussion. She was reviewing, amongst others, Alison Fell's first novel, *Every Move You Make*, and one entitled *Hannah at Thirty-Five or How to Survive Divorce* by Anabel Donald. In her review Bailey voices the opinion, heard with monotonous regularity over the past few years, that feminism has in a sense done its work. It isn't needed any longer and women do themselves no good by inculcating a ghetto mentality:

> It might be time to mention to women authors that just because they happen to be women they aren't obliged to deal always in experience specific to women.
>
> (*Guardian*, 22 March 1984)

Can you imagine anyone saying the equivalent to Wilbur Smith, John Mortimer, Kingsley Amis, Salman Rushdie, Bruce Chatwin? Of course not, for men's experience of, and fictional representation of, their lives *are* the world: life, how it is.

We discussed the way the media had reported on feminism in general, and how the literary media reviewed women's writing and interviewed women writers. In 1984, the general tone was one of bemused tolerance, generally shading into outright paranoia, as, for example, in the case of Sheba's publication of *For Ourselves*, edited by Anja Meulenbelt. Women writers are very frequently accused of writing only for women, as if women were not a legitimate audience and as if men were regularly chastised for over-attention to male concerns and issues. It was rare, even when women writers such as Margaret Atwood, Paule Marshall, Doris

Lessing etc. were profiled, to have those interviews conducted by women. There seemed to be a need to rescue the few good women artists from the feminists. As the 1980s progressed, the term 'post-feminism' was coined, and preoccupation with it grew. Men, and a considerable number of women too, claimed, not to be anti-feminist, but that feminism was old-hat. Equality between the sexes had arrived and feminism was an anachronism, especially in its more 'strident' forms.

The areas that most stimulated our discussion were concerned with the responsibility which came with success and with being identified in some way as representatives or leaders. We noted, too, in that context how in political action collective anonymity and solidarity seemed more possible, as Angry Women or the Greenham Common Women had shown, than in creative work. We talked about the need we had for stars, and how calling them heroines or role models made them somehow more acceptable, to ourselves as well as to other feminists.

Evaluating the course, students commented on the challenge it was to hold political and literary questions together. The stress on personal experience was welcomed, as a way of making the issues accessible. The way we taught it, the students had a brief introduction to a range of material and writers. The advantage of doing it that way is that you give students a set of questions and concerns which they can then extend into their own reading, and you give them an indication of the range of writing they could go on to pursue. With adult women students, who may have many demands on their time or irregular periods of free time, this is a positive way to use the time; it also gives students something to take away and work on independently.

2

THE PERSONAL

Throughout courses like 'Feminism and Writing', certain themes and areas of interest constantly surfaced. These were evident in the writing, and were picked up and reinforced as concerns by the women participating. In particular, issues around various types of relationships – between mothers and daughters, between lovers, between friends – and the ways in which they impinged on each other, presented themselves more and more not only as literary themes, but also as areas of conflict that remained unresolved in our own lives.

The demand to examine such issues led us to rethink the ways in which we organised our courses, and the roles of tutor and student. We gradually shifted from a tutor-organised and directed model of teaching to a more participatory, student-led model, encouraging and developing students' skills as readers, interpreters, critics and presenters. This shift reflected changes in the ways in which women writers were operating under the influence of feminism, bringing together different forms of writing as tools for the exploration of ideas, rather than as finished products in themselves.

This shift also provided a way of approaching issues that are intrinsically personal and central to women's lives. Women writers weave the threads of their own lives into their work (a good example is Adrienne Rich's *Of Woman Born* (Virago 1977) – a mixture of memoir and history written to explore subjectively and objectively the experience of motherhood). Women readers bring their lives to bear on writing, through interpretation, criticism and enjoyment. Personal concerns – the ways in which we lead our lives and relate to each other – are the bedrock of feminist thought.

Looking back on the multi-faceted nature of a series of courses which we presented on the theme of 'Mothers and Daughters'

humour abortion poetry letters myths/realities of motherhood

being a lesbian mother
being a lesbian daughter   diaries

                                            cultural differences
                       history   Black women

writing   mothers in society   mothers/daughters & the Women's Movement

         infertility   Jewish women
religions   grandmothers   workshops
         class   abuse   AIDS   race   daughters of fathers

   changes   separation
                silences/   painting
                creativity   Mothers &   mothering daughters
fiction   Daughters   age   visual images
                              -being a mother
mother/daughter aspects of sexuality -being a daughter   media images
                              conflict & resolution
   mothering sons   disabled mothers/disabled daughters

choosing not to have children   non-biological parenting   artificial insemination
                                                                      motherless
   in vitro fertilisation   daughters
               autobiography   motherhood & work
polemic   fostering/adoption   pregnancy & childbirth

choosing to have children

Brainstorming 'Mothers and Daughters'

32

(encapsulated in the diagram on page 32), for example, we can discern some of the advantages and difficulties of working in this way. We chose 'Mothers and Daughters' as a title because we are all mothers and/or daughters. It was not, however, intended to discriminate against other familial relationships, particularly those with fathers, sons, and grandparents, and we attempted to incorporate those relationships into the courses. With some writers, such as Sylvia Plath and Virginia Woolf, it is impossible to consider mother–daughter relationships without also looking at fathers and daughters (and, in Plath's case, mothers and sons), and although the mother–daughter relationship often appears to predominate, those between daughters and fathers, mothers and sons, and grandchildren and grandparents can prove highly significant and challenging.

The centrality of the mother–daughter relationship within many of our lives engenders some of the difficulties encountered in courses dealing with the personal. It can be an area of great pain, of loss or guilt or conflict or dissatisfaction, as well as being a cause for celebration and fulfilment. The values society places on the role of mother (highly valued/badly paid; success assumed and taken for granted/failure excoriated and damned) increase the pressure it sustains; our own senses of duty, responsibility and inadequacy bear down powerfully on our views of motherhood. Mothers are not praised for successfully raising daughters, but they are heavily blamed for 'bad' sons; next to that of wife, the role of mother must carry with it the most potential for opprobrium (look at the supposed 'causes' of mass-murderer Peter Sutcliffe's criminality). Moreover, whether the role of mother involves daughters and/or sons, it is always tacitly regarded as a one-way operation, all power and influence emanating from the mother, with daughters and sons as apparently passive, empty vessels over which she has absolute control.

Similarly, as daughters we may experience dissatisfaction, lack of fulfilment, a sense of guilt, or anger, in our relationships with our mothers. Sometimes these feelings may be reinforced, sometimes resolved, by becoming mothers ourselves, or being involved in parenting roles. On the other hand, relations between mothers and daughters can be extremely close and supportive, maybe the primary relationship of our lives, and thus expose us to the searing experience of loss and grief. In addition, daughters face the conflict of societal expectations, which mainly emphasise duty and obligation, and assume a caring facility which can often become a terrible burden – this assumption being implicit in the present Conservative government's notions of community and family care.

Within the realm of the personal, one might assume a universality of experience around the major themes. But, as we have suggested elsewhere, these are precisely the sorts of areas where difference can be most usefully discovered and explored. Again, to take examples from 'Mothers and Daughters', we had to consider our own and our students' often strongly held beliefs and differing experiences of the subject, discussion of which may lead to conflict and hostility. One woman stopped coming to a 'Mothers and Daughters' course because she felt attacked for her belief that her children should be brought up in conventional gender roles. Other difficulties may arise in discussion between mothers and non-mothers, between biological and non-biological parents, between heterosexual and lesbian mothers. Similarly, a course which does not provide a wide cultural representation may exclude women who feel that their experiences are being ignored.

At their best, courses focusing on the personal can cut across the barriers of oppression, of place and of time, and can validate the various personal and literary experiences and development of tutors and students alike. Such courses offer the opportunity for creating an integrated curriculum, drawing on writing and other cultural forms from around the world. In the course described in this chapter, we attempted to engage with the themes of love, sex and friendship as expressed by a variety of writers and reflected through our own lived experience.

'LOVE, SEX AND FRIENDSHIP': AN EXPLORATION OF WOMEN'S WRITING

This course explored the assumption that women's writing concerns itself with relationships, primarily between lovers, and that for many women readers, fiction was a place to get 'lessons on life'.

We wanted to look at heterosexuality and lesbianism, consider the way that ageing determined these relationships and to see whether feminism had produced any writing which explored

women's friendships. Part of our interest, too, lay in exploring
the relationship between love, sex and friendship. The boundaries
and definitions of the terms are both socially and individually
arrived at. We saw feminism as something which had the potential
to pose a radical challenge to these terms and, during the last decade,
had often thrown them into crisis. We wanted to problematise the
apparent choices women had in their personal lives and to see
how fiction reflected and made sense of those choices, changes and
challenges.

We began with a brief introduction to the course aims and the
books we would be looking at in detail: *A Reckoning* by May
Sarton; *Cactus* by Anna Wilson; and *Every Move You Make* by
Alison Fell. We divided the group into pairs and discussed the
following questions:

1 Are we right in our assumption that much women's writing
   concerns itself with relationships and the emotional life?
2 Is this why you read it?
3 Are there any books that have been particularly important to
   you in relation to choices or decisions concerning your intimate
   relationships? How, and why?

In the discussion, it became clear that women differentiated the
types of women writers that they read and that a number of women
had only recently started to read women writers at all. It was felt
that the first assumption was correct, but equally that this was often
used to trivialise women's writing and reading. We spent some time
untangling the preoccupations of romance, with its often attendant
cliched characterisation and writing, from women's interest in the
reactions between people, their preoccupation with psychological
detail and dynamics.

We found that the women's reasons for reading were fascinating.
This was a group of committed readers, therefore the pattern
and expectation of the reading was quite different from those of
women studying literature, much of whose reading is required
rather than chosen, or for women within adult basic education,
reading at a much slower rate and only slowly progressing to
complete novels. These women read for pleasure, and came to
the course in order to expand that pleasure. The commonest
reason for reading was the exchange of ideas and stimulation it
offered. This was particularly important for women who were
at home, either with children or because they were long-term

unemployed. Coming to the course was, for them, a way of extending the stimulus books already gave them. It did so in ways that were also important socially. Going out to classes was a more accessible, and acceptable, way of socialising for women than, for instance, going to the pub. It was also a sociability which wasn't based on children, and as such was very welcomed by women at home with small children. The course offered the opportunity to share and to participate in intellectual and personal insights. Women who were interested in feminism looked to their reading, fiction and non-fiction, for the elaboration of political ideas into familiar situations, as well as using it as a way to learn about the lives and histories of women in completely different situations.

Many of the women spoke about the enormous curiosity they had about anything to do with women's lives and writing after years spent reading male writers. The relative scarcity of books which featured friendships between women was clear to us all. One woman spoke about how she used fiction to balance her own life. She meant by this that she looked to writing for a reflection of her own situation, but also to see it in a new light. She wanted her dilemmas and inadequacies taken seriously and the reassurance of seeing other women confront and deal with them, even if it was in ways that she personally wouldn't find helpful. This seemed to strike a chord with everyone. It may suggest a utilitarian approach to reading but that would be wrong. What seemed to matter most was that a book – or a character, or a predicament – moved us, at an intellectual or emotional level.

We brainstormed around the words love, sex and friendship. This was the list we got:

Love	Sex	Friendship
Empty	And love	Strength
Abstraction	Closeness	Timeless
Sometimes	Pleasure	Solid
Confidence	Giving	Important
Unreal	Taking	Fun
Lovely	Greedy	Easiness
Insecurity	Scary	Plentiful
Excitement	Wonderful	Changing
Terror	Secrets	Security

Had the list been constructed anonymously, it may well have been very different. In generating a discussion from the lists, we posed two questions: first, what are common to these experiences; second, what is distinct about them. Out of this, we arrived at a series of problematic areas which were as follows:

1 Expressing emotions; their power for the person who has them and for the person in receipt of them.
2 The reasons why we are attracted to some people and not to others, given the potential to be attracted by all and any. The ways in which attraction is often strong towards people who do not reciprocate; this last was commoner in sex and love than in friendships.
3 The mingling of self-expression and self-fulfilment with sex and love, the failure of ourselves and others to acknowledge that much of our selfhood comes through friendships; to what extent has the women's liberation movement reversed the traditional pattern of women reserving intimacy for the 'loved one' and maintaining shallow friendships with other women; was this assumption about women's emotional life ever true anyway?
4 Has the women's liberation movement changed our sense of rights and responsibilities in the sexual and emotional spheres of our lives? Have other factors been at work, and, if so, which?
5 Are love, sex and friendship fixed and absolute categories? Is it more accurate to talk about them each in terms of continuums and/or discourses?

With each of these areas, we were interested in the question of choice. What does the responsibility of knowing yourself and your needs involve? How do you move from knowing what you want to acting on it? What factors determine the choices we have and make?

We agreed that there was some choice about the families and communities we make for ourselves, but that it exists within the limits of:

1 Our emotional and sexual formation inside and outside the family.
2 Our material circumstances – money, time, job, where we live, children etc.

3 Our taste and personality, the irrational.

These very general, and sometimes very intimate, discussions served as guides for the following weeks' discussions about the particular texts. They provided a set of reference points for the group, as well as a framework of questions for the literary works we moved onto. It would be possible to ask students to read more widely on the subject of women, sex and sexuality from writers such as Adrienne Rich, Lynne Segal, Ann Snitow etc.

Over the next three weeks, we introduced each of the selected novels in turn along with relevant questions for discussion. Later, we wanted to involve the students in a much more practical way. First, we asked students to work as a group analysing reviews of two of the novels we were discussing. Then we selected two quite different stories and asked them to work, in groups, towards a critical account of that story.

We chose May Sarton's *A Reckoning* because it seemed to delve into and weigh such a variety of relationships in one woman's life that we felt there were a number of points of entry for our own preoccupations and concerns. The heightening of Laura Spelman's sense of her connections with others as a result of learning she has terminal lung cancer renders the issues more clearly and with more urgency than usual. In addition, it seemed important to begin with an older woman's experiences, to challenge the chauvinism of youth in its attempt to monopolise deep feeling and emotional conflicts. It was also an opportunity, as these classes often were, to introduce a new author to students and to take stock of a new publication. May Sarton has been writing and publishing novels, poetry and journals for more than fifty years. Virginia Woolf in her diary notes meetings with her as a young woman. She is, however, far more widely known in North America than she is in Britain. The Women's Press has, since 1983, started to reissue some of her work. We were also interested to see how Sarton's use of the concept of death, rather than romance, worked as an orchestrator of plot.

We introduced the session with a summary of the book which highlighted points of particular interest, and concluded with questions for discussion. After allowing some time for a general discussion of responses to the novel, we suggested the following as areas to look at in more detail.

1 Does it take a lifetime to recognise and resolve the conflicts and contradictions of our lives?

2 *A Reckoning* deals centrally with relations between women but would not be classified as a lesbian novel. Are we arriving at a time when relations with women can be central to our lives?
3 The ways in which the novel details extreme tensions between chosen and unchosen relationships forces the question concerning where the real connections lie – family, friends, lovers, work? How useful is this way of looking at relationships?
4 What are the implications for the novel's structure of making imminent death its organising feature?
5 What other writing can you think of that addresses women's friendship? Does it contradict or complement May Sarton?

A Reckoning begins with Laura's immediate, and consistent, response to approaching death:

> In the few seconds of silence it had become clear that she was going to have to reckon with almost everything in a new way. 'It is then to be a reckoning' and Laura realised that at this moment she felt closer to Mozart and Chekhov than she did to her own sister. 'I shall not pretend that this is not so. There isn't time. The time I have left is for the real connections.'
>
> (Sarton 1984: 10)

Before she can live out this decision, however, she has to be clear what the real connections are, and the action of the novel is to take us through the very varied and extensive relationships she has had and continues to have in her search to confirm her real connections. In the course of the search, we are brought up against ideas which challenge our expectations of dying and of intimacy and family. At first, Laura approaches the reckoning as a way of drawing together and catching up the threads of her life, but the movement of the novel is, in fact, to let them go. The book is steeped in genteel and cultured intellectualism to such an extent that at times it cloys and infuriates. Money eases Laura's last months of life in a way few people suddenly struck down by a terminal illness could possibly expect. It also frees her to operate on the emotional plane, unhampered by the compromise of material considerations. And, for our class at any rate, the references to music and to the choicest wine and food began to grate after a while. This can be a problem which overshadows the radical conclusions that the book reaches for. Ways of dealing with this might include confronting it

directly and discussing what sorts of alternatives exist for women
in less privileged situations and the consequences of that.

Laura is sixty. She is located through many social relationships.
She is Charlie's widow, the mother of two sons, Brook and Ben,
and a daughter, Daisy. Brook lives near by, married to Ann. Ben,
whose homosexuality is known but unacknowledged between
them, lives on the West Coast. Daisy, with whom Laura has
had a tempestuous relationship, lives in New York with her male
lover. Laura is grandmother to Brook and Ann's children, Laurie
and Charley.

Laura's mother, Sybille, is still alive although senile and living
in a home. Her sisters are still alive: Jo, the eldest, unmarried and
wrapped up in her job as the president of a small women's college;
Daphne, the youngest and always most beautiful, as well as the
one most inattentive to her beauty, works in an animal shelter in
New York, the mistress for twenty years of a married man. An
aunt, Minna, to whom she has always been close is still alive, as is
a cousin, Hope, whose devotion to Sybille is, and always has been,
far greater than Laura's own. Laura, then, is set firmly within the
family, in all its complexities and rivalries and its opportunities for
support and conflict, for hope and regret.

Preoccupied as Laura is with unravelling the threads, past and
present, which bind her to the family, and the shifting understanding she has of that family, she is also concerned with other
relationships. Of her friendships, it is the one with Ella, dating
from her youth, which haunts her now and, in a story-book
ending, Ella arrives from England just days before her death.
She also makes new friendships, or, perhaps more accurately, has
much deeper emotional experiences with people new to her circle:
Harriet Moors, a new author she encourages just before she decides
to give up her job as a fiction editor; Jim Goodwin, her doctor and
Mary O'Brien, the live-in nurse she has in preference to care by her
family or in hospital.

Animals, too, figure largely in Laura's world. She has a dog,
Grindle, and a cat, Sasha, with whom she experiences a simplicity
that sustains her amidst, and acts as a refuge from, the complica-
tions of personal encounters.

The lines between overt lesbianism and passionate friendship lie
at the heart of the novel, although they are overarched by the more
powerful relationship that exists between mothers and daughters.
Sybille, the powerful and dazzling mother, has destroyed her

daughter's relationships with women. The message from *A Reck-oning* about mother–daughter relationships is that it is not possible for a mother and her daughter(s) to lay to rest the antagonisms that fracture them both. At the end of the novel, at the moment of her death, Laura chooses Ella. Although Daisy is in the house, she asks her to stay away, but not so far that she cannot hear her playing her guitar and singing. Laura and Daisy can acknowledge their difficulties, and this is as far as progress can go.

Laura comes to recognise that the ways in which women have been important to her have not been given their full due. It is the discussions with Harriet that bring it home. She questions the ways she has behaved towards her homosexual son, Ben, and to her sister. But there is a deeper reverberation:

> one of the deepest and most nourishing, in some ways more than my marriage, good as that was, had been a passionate friendship with a woman . . . Women's feeling for one another has been a buried world for so long, a cause of fear and shame.
>
> (Sarton 1984: 143)

The taunt, or fear, of lesbianism has been one of the more powerful weapons used against women's friendships. The implications for lesbian identity and experience are clearly negative, but they are for any kind of friendship and commitment between women. *A Reckoning* does not reach any conclusions, but it brings the questions into the open very clearly, through the constantly reit-erated theme of exploring what it means to be a woman. The range of women characters in the novel set out some of the options, but none of them is allowed to be the ideal. The hardships involved in each are detailed, as well as the compromises and the pleasures. Between them, Sybille, Minna, Jo, Laura, Daphne, Ann, Ella, Daisy, Harriet and Hope span generations and relations to family and work. In discussion with Laura, or in her reflections, a thorough consideration of the choices available to middle-class white women becomes possible.

Women have been kept from each other, and have suffered for it, is the place this novel reaches. All of Laura's unfinished business is with women. Her father and her husband barely impinge at all, they have an air of being both benign and irrelevant. Women are both the loose ends and the means to her own unfinished self. What is very powerful and moving about *A Reckoning* is that the conclusions

Laura reaches at the end in many ways contradict and diminish her life. Yet instead of despair, bitterness or regret she faces her finding with enthusiasm and excitement: women's lives are at last coming right. It is with Aunt Minna and Ella she shares that excitement.

> however original and powerful a woman may have been – and as surely you are – we have allowed ourselves to be caught in all sorts of stereotypes. What is a woman meant to be, anyway? We don't think of men as 'meant to be' primarily married and fathers, do we? . . . women have been in a queer way locked away from one another in a man's world. The perspective has been from there.
>
> (Sarton 1984: 191–3)

Laura takes great pains to detach what she is saying from a simple interpretation that would tie it to sex. The connections between women that involve sexual and emotional love have been repressed, but she is reaching after a more complex sense of fulfilment. Talking with Ella, Laura realises for the first time how cleverly her mother manipulated them both. Although Ella had been sent away, she refused to go, but the

> atmosphere of scandal, worse, of sin, around any such relationship at that time! We had been poisoned by the whole ethos, taught to be mortally afraid of what our bodies tried to teach us.
>
> (Sarton 1984: 252)

Laura and Ella were not lovers in that sense, and, although they shared much that was essential, they never got to what Laura has decided is the most important thing in the world.

> Communion. Something women are only beginning to tap, to understand, a kind of tenderness towards each other as women. Just as Sybille was, we have been afraid of it.
>
> (Sarton 1984: 252)

Although she has lived as a lesbian throughout her life, and much of her poetry and autobiographical writing deals with that experience, May Sarton rarely centres her novels on lesbianism. *Mrs Stevens Hears the Mermaids Singing*, published in 1965, is the one of her few novels which deals directly with the experience of acknowledging and living with lesbianism. Many of her novels are set within, and explore dimensions of, heterosexuality. Her journals, however, deal frankly with her life as a lesbian, including the pain of caring for a latterly senile lover until her death. Her later novels, such as *As We Are Now* and *The Magnificent Spinster*, as well as *A Reckoning*, tackle women's friendship, sometimes in the context of lesbianism but never lesbianism in its own terms, until *The Education of Harriet Hatfield* (1990).

The second book we selected, *Cactus* by Anna Wilson, nicely counterpointed May Sarton. This novel, too, is concerned with friendships between women, but women who define themselves as lesbians. It also looks back to the kind of relationships possible for women in the 1950s and the mid-1970s by comparing two pairs of women, Dee and Ann and Beatrice and Eleanor.

Published in 1980, *Cactus* is Anna Wilson's first novel, and was brought out by Onlywomen Press, the only lesbian-feminist publishing company in Britain. Much of the lesbian, and lesbian-feminist, writing available in this country originates elsewhere, usually in North America. *Cactus* is important in setting out the preoccupations and assumptions of a lesbian existence rooted in this country. While it reflects the privileged class background of its author, the novel also charts the more general preoccupations of lesbian–feminism at that time. Central to the novel, and to lesbian politics of the late 1970s, were questions of community, separatism and the political nature of lesbianism. The questions we asked students to think about and discuss were as follows:

1 Is this novel what you expected from a lesbian novel?
2 What are the advantages and disadvantages of comparing Dee and Ann with Eleanor and Bea?
3 What observations and conclusions are reached about separatism?
4 Does the novel confirm or challenge the idea that lesbianism is essentially a political act? What are your views?

The novel opens with the innocent, almost accidental coming together of Eleanor and Bea, friends who work together and together go on holiday. They have booked a cottage to sleep two, not realising it will only have one bed. Sharing the bed, their desire for each other surfaces and is mutual. At this stage, it is Bea who is reckless, wanting to kiss Eleanor in public, not caring about being seen. Eleanor is conscious of the day-to-day realities, and plans a life with Bea that involves escapes and disguises:

We can live quietly, in the country perhaps – and to the world we shall be just spinsters, best left alone. But to ourselves, we shall be everything, be open.

(Wilson 1980: 3)

Although Bea doesn't like the idea of hiding what she is and does, at the same time she is insistent that no one must know about them. Later, it is Bea who ends their relationship, accepting the pressure to marry and conform. She is uncomfortable at the way Eleanor wants to assert their relationship on its own terms: to offer people the chance to accept or reject them.

'It's not recognised, Nellie,' she said at last, despairing of an explanation. 'It's not something that anyone thinks that you do.'

(Wilson 1980: 8)

Bea marries and has two daughters, and stays at home until they leave. Eleanor moves out to the country, lives alone and runs a greengrocer's shop. They maintain contact with each other, but do not visit.

Ann and Dee have moved out to the country from the city, living together and testing out their commitment to each other. It has been a difficult decision to make, and throughout the course of the novel the decision becomes harder to sustain. At the end of the novel they decide to move back to the city. The difficulties are rooted partly in their relation to each other, balancing each other's needs for independence and dependence, and partly in their social existence as lesbians. Ann says:

Look, if I want to go back to the city it's not you I want to leave, it's this desert. I'm tired of always having to use cactus skills, as if that's all there ever was for lesbians in the world – drink in the fleeting support of the ghetto, grow a thick skin to withstand the heat of a hostile environment, go sit in the desert for a year drinking your juices meanly.

(Wilson 1980: 22)

Dee gets a job at Eleanor's shop, which causes some friction in her relationship with Ann. Meanwhile Bea, restless and lacking in self-confidence after her children have left home, decides on impulse to visit Eleanor. The disruption the visit causes to Eleanor's self-sufficient life style reverberates into Ann and Dee's life too.

Bea goes back and Eleanor withdraws the tentative moves towards friendship she had extended towards Dee. The interaction between the four women allow us to weigh the question of choices, for lesbians and for heterosexual women.

It also problematises the whole area of friendship between lesbians. There is much mutual suspicion between Ann and Eleanor and between Dee and Beatrice. Some of it stems from jealousy and a fear of losing the loved one, as do Dee's anxieties about Ann wanting to move back to the city. Some of it, though, stems from a sense of being judged and found wanting by other women, especially other lesbians, about the way they live their lives. The novel seems to suggest that the critical scrutiny given to lesbian lives from the heterosexual world is extended and heightened between lesbians. The demands that lesbians make on each other are high indeed. This is most clearly articulated in the argument that develops between Dee and Beatrice:

> 'Perhaps those that did it then did it for less upright reasons than you,'

argues Beatrice, about the women living as lesbians in the 1950s. Dee rounds on her,

> 'Too warped for anything else, you mean? . . . And we none of us do it by choice? I do, Beatrice, I wouldn't bolster up your heterosexual world at any price – not for any lack of ability to enjoy sex with men, or their company, or their money, or their protection.'
>
> (Wilson 1980: 124)

The third novel read and discussed by the whole group was one which took its starting-points from the impact of feminism upon heterosexuality. It was *Every Move You Make* by Alison Fell, published in 1984 (by Virago). Told in the first person, the novel provides an account of London's counter-culture of left politics, squats and actions and feminist struggles during the mid-1970s. June Guthrie, a working-class Scot who married young and finally makes the break from domesticity and motherhood, is the leading character. She is the pivot of the various relationships the novel explores: her friendship with Vi, her relationship with Vi's ex-lover, Matt, her son, Andrew, and the two relationships with men, Phil and Jed, she tries to balance after she first arrives in London.

The questions we thought would be helpful for students to think about were these:

1 Is the alternative to sexual relationships always such a loneliness? Can we de-centre such relationships; do we want to?
2 Can we define what the need for love is, the need for relationships beyond friendship? Are the words we use to describe this area of experience – relationship, lover, friend, friendship – the best ones?
3 Why is it so hard to write about sexual passion? Is it harder to talk about it than to write about it? Is it unacceptable or frightening, or both? How well does Alison Fell do it?
4 What does the novel present as the common ground of friendships between women? Do you agree that these are its bases?
5 What does the novel suggest that women get from relationships with men? Do you think this is enough?

We discussed first what the novel had to say about friendship. Early on, the sense that friendship is second rate is established:

> I was convulsed with discontent. All I did with my life was work on the magazine, see to Andrew, visit women friends. Living at the minimum: it felt like a disease.
>
> (Fell 1984: 9)

Vi is June's oldest friend, and comes in for an astonishingly hard time from her during the course of the novel. June resents Vi's demands upon her, and sees all her intimacy as a demand.

> Comradeship, after all, we already had. I could hardly see that there was time for more
>
> (Fell 1984: 37)

she says at one point, and later

> Why should she save up all this self-exposure for me?
>
> (Fell 1984: 36)

In the novel, friendships with women are never a positive force in themselves, they either arise in the course of some other shared activity, and remain dependent upon that, or are generated through some sort of opposition. They also lack equality. June is unwilling to reciprocate Vi's confidences or to accept her support during her own crisis times. Perhaps more significantly, June is admired to the point of hero-worship by both Mike and Vi. Although she expresses a degree of contempt for this, there is also the suggestion that she enjoys, if not expects, it. The main thread in Vi and June's relationship during the course of the novel is Matt, and that is calculated to bring out the competitive, bitter streak in it. When Vi and June meet for the first time since June's relationship with Matt began, she listens irritably to Vi's anger and disappointment, not with Matt but with her. June cannot hear the truth of Vi's accusation: 'It's the men who have the magic, isn't it?'

The other woman June has most involvement with is Mike, a lesbian she has known from her days at the Women's Centre, who also works for Womanright. Mike has a kind of fascination for June, but it is the fascination of the awful. She cannot understand, and is uncomfortable with, lesbianism.

The whole subject gave me gooseflesh.

(Fell 1984: 209)

Unlike Mike, June thinks and feels in oppositions; a man makes her feel feminine, she says, and cannot understand Mike saying she feels neither feminine nor masculine with her lover, simply female. June says she doesn't know the meaning of that word and mumbles on about lesbianism as a choice, for which she sees no grounds in herself, or

whether it all comes down to that mother stuff, in the end.

(Fell 1984: 210)

June's friendships with men are always sexual, with the exception of Reuben, a therapist that Vi and Mike take her to at her lowest ebb. There is an incredible amount of tension in her sexual life. Because men are not capable of understanding what she wants and satisfying her sexually, she withdraws from them. She keeps her sexual pleasure for herself, in masturbation, rather than sharing it with her lovers. At the same time, she needs and wants her men. She is in the grip of passion, especially where Matt is concerned.

Powerfully, the novel poses the questions of what sex is for women, what it is in itself and what it buys for them. June has a contradictory pull towards and away from sex. On the one hand she wants complete oblivion from it, and demands a dispersal out of which will come a new ordering of her world. At the same time, she fears sex precisely for its ability to generate chaos.

> I was afraid, yes I was afraid he would push and prod me down into that wordless darkness where countless invasions and penetrations were possible, where there were so few boundaries against the leakage of one into another.
>
> Trust? Already my skin was becoming too thin. And where did I end and the world begin?
>
> (Fell 1984: 169)

Sex is often presented as a sort of battle-ground, a case of what they each do to and with each other. Only very occasionally is there the suggestion of togetherness, of a meeting and sharing together. Even when the sex is good, and they are harmonious there is a pull away from each other.

> I wanted to go home, to spread myself luxuriously in my empty house . . . to lie in a solitary bath, and love him from there.
>
> (Fell 1984: 165)

The space between men and women seems enormous, and in no way lessened by Matt's continual sniping at June's friends, politics, work and past. Despite that, she experiences a compelling need for him. Sex is presented as a threat to the stability of life: their relationship causes tension and conflict in all the other areas of their lives: with her son, Andrew, with her friends Vi and Mike, with his friend Marshall and at her place of work. The novel is very bleak in its account of contemporary sexual possibilities for heterosexual women. Bleak, too, is the suggestion that feminism makes worse rather than better the problems and their solutions.

The novel raised a number of areas for our discussion, many of which we got into simply through asking 'Did you like this novel?' Many of the group had had personal experience of the same politics and period as the one written about and, to a greater or lesser extent, had faced similar conflicts in their lives. It was interesting to discuss how far they agreed with Alison Fell. Interesting, too, was how many of us had found the way the novel was written compelling and pleasing even while we disagreed and were angered by some of the implications of what was being said.

In this course, we were trying to encourage our students to take a more active part in discussions and to practise a more critical reading of the text than is sometimes achieved when the focus rests too much with the content of writing, as the spur to discussions about experience. A useful way of proceeding into this area of judgement and assessment seemed to be through reviews.

Having looked in detail at *Cactus* and *Every Move You Make,* we studied how they had been reviewed on publication and discussed the nature and scope of reviewing. This began to turn us towards questions of taste and accomplishment. We wanted to generalise from particular opinions, and to show the way ideas cluster around certain novels and novelists.

In preparation, we wrote to the publishers of the two novels and asked them to send us photostats of the various reviews received. We made extra copies of these and then divided the group into two, one took *Cactus* and the other *Every Move You Make* and we read through and discussed the reviews. Our final task was to present our findings back to the other group. These activities were spread over a three-week period.

The questions we used to guide us through the material were as follows:

1 What is the purpose of a review?
2 Who writes them?
3 Does the reviewer assume a particular audience for the book and for the review?
4 What other books are reviewed at the same time, how much space does your novel get?
5 How would you describe and explain the differences between reviews?
   Do men and women review books differently?
6 Do the reviews reflect your own experience or impressions of the book?
   Have they clarified or changed your views?
7 What sort of context does the reviewer put the book into?
8 Does being published by a feminist or lesbian press seem to influence the reviewers?
9 Could we write a review?

The following sessions were interesting ones. The approach, breaking up the pattern of one of the tutors introducing a session with a short talk followed by questions and discussions, provided more opportunities for people's emerging confidence to express itself. There seemed to be much more activity going on in the session;

people worked together, worked much harder and spoke of a sense of accomplishment at the end of it. Presenting our findings back to the other group was difficult, as most members of the class felt shy and inhibited. Both tutors had made it clear at the outset that they would not be the reporters. But because the members had coalesced as a group, they were able to support each other in their presentations.

For the final weeks of the course we continued working in two groups. We selected two short stories which illustrated and problematised the themes we had been discussing. 'Till September Petronella' by Jean Rhys was chosen partly in response to a student request.

The story is set in July 1914 and told in the first person by Petronella, an artist's model eking out a hand-to-mouth existence in Bloomsbury. She is invited down to a country cottage by Marston, an artist, who shares the cottage with a musician friend, Julian. There is another woman, Frankie, with him. Petronella recognises her from a dubious night club they both frequent, but they do not acknowledge that they know each other until later, when they are alone.

The trip is not a success. Petronella is attracted by Julian and spends a lot of the time avoiding Marston. After only a few days, a row develops in which Julian accuses Petronella of being fifth-rate and preventing Marston from working. She leaves the cottage and decides to go back to London, but has left without her bag or belongings. She is picked up by a farmer, who sees that she is looked after and given a meal. Later, he tries to persuade her to agree to an arrangement.

She refuses his offer, but convinces him to drive her back to the cottage to collect her belongings and then to take her to the station. Her parting from Marston, who will see her again in September, is amicable enough. The deliberate dating of the story, just a few weeks before the outbreak of the First World War, adds an irony to this promise. September, when it comes, will never be the same again for any of them. Marston's expectations of Petronella are as low as are her own of life. The story is written in a melancholic, cynical vein. She is too conscious of time passing and with it her chances of success, love and security fading as her looks and figure begin to age. What financial independence she has comes from her ability to manipulate men. When she reaches London, she picks up another man:

And everything was exactly as I had expected. The knowing waiters, the touch of the ice-cold wine glass, the red plush chairs, the food you don't notice, the gold framed mirror, the bed in the room beyond that always looks as if its ostentatious whiteness hides dinginess.

(Rhys 1968: 33)

The elegiac tone of the story, its muffled sadness about what life can possibly hold in store for Petronella, can be traced back not just to the very real limits imposed by her life style and the ways in which her exploitation by men makes up the only chance of freedom she has, but to the loss of her friendship with Estelle. Estelle once had a room in the same house as Petronella, and envied Petronella's poise:

She had everything so cut and dried, she walked the tightrope so beautifully, not even knowing she was walking it.

(Rhys 1968: 9)

Estelle has returned to Paris at the beginning of the story and, by its end, Petronella is sure she will never come back.

We gave separate questions to each group. Those for Jean Rhys's story were:

1 How does the author, if she does, write about love, sex and friendship?
2 This story was first published in 1960 but was almost certainly written some years previously. What sort of context would you place it in?
3 How does it compare with the other writing we've considered?
4 Can this story be read as feminist?
5 How accessible is this story?
6 How do short stories differ from novels?
7 Do you like the story? Give reasons for your answer.

We felt there was a tension in the way Jean Rhys wrote about love and sex. On the one hand, there was a deeply romantic notion, expressed by Petronella writing and hiding love letters she would never send, and revealed in the language she uses to describe Estelle's room, which she compares to a book:

you read one page of it or even one phrase of it, and then you gobble up all the rest and go about in a dream for weeks afterwards, for months afterwards – perhaps all your life, who

51

knows? – surrounded by those six hundred and fifty pages
. . . it is alive, this book, and it grows in your head. 'The
house I was living in when I read that book', you think.

(Rhys 1968: 10)

On the other hand, her approach is realistic and unsentimental.
Women without any other means of support must be supported by
men, and their survival skill is to extract the maximum of support,
usually financial, but not exclusively so, for the minimum loss of
self. Sex is always implicit in the story and quite detached from
romance. It is as much a job of work as being a chorus girl or an
artist's model.

When she writes about friendship, Jean Rhys shows its impos-
sibility between men and women. The problem is not just women's
economic dependence on men, it is more deeply rooted than that,
in men's fear and hatred of women:

> 'You ghastly cross between a barmaid and a chorus girl,'
> he said. 'You female spider,' he said; 'You've been laughing
> at him for weeks,' he said, 'jeering at him, sniggering at
> him. Stopping him from working – the best painter in this
> damnable island, the only one in my opinion.'
>
> (Rhys 1968: 21)

Friendships between women are constrained, too. Estelle suggests
a supportive and a positive relationship, but it is over as the story
opens. Frankie and Petronella are suspicious of each other and
forced to compete for male favours. In a world where women
must snare men to survive, they walk a fine line with each other
as allies and enemies. The need to compete for men also puts the
pressure on women to retain their youth and beauty for as long as
possible. Other women become the standard against which men,
and women, judge. The uncomfortable relationship Petronella has
to her own body is carried through the story by her critical remarks
about other women:

> You saw so many old women, or women who seemed
> old, peering at the vegetables in the Camden Town market,
> looking at you with hatred, or blankly, as though they had
> forgotten your language, and talked another one. 'My God,' I
> would think, 'I hope I never live to be old. Anyway, however
> old I get, I'll never let my hair go grey.'
>
> (Rhys 1968: 10)

When we compared this story with the novels we had read, it at first seemed very different. The lack of resources these women had and the inescapable meshing of their lives with those of men seemed peculiar to a period in history where women, particularly of the working class, had very limited opportunities. We were aware, too, of how women moved between classes, depending on the men they were with. In discussion, though, we found a similarity between Jean Rhys and Alison Fell that surprised us. The similarities lay in the despairing tones with which relationships between men and women were discussed. It seemed that in *Every Move You Make* it was easier for women to sustain themselves financially without recourse to men, and certainly there was no need for the characters to engage in the casual prostitution forced on Petronella and Frankie by economic necessity. But emotional independence was another matter altogether. In some respects, it seemed that Alison Fell's women were more, rather than less, emotionally fixated on men who were causing them damage.

Moving on, we had difficulty in deciding whether the story was feminist or not. Judged by the standards of our own time, and the conclusions it reaches, we felt not. But works from an earlier period have to be read in the context of their own times and in that respect, and looking at the content of the story, we felt an argument could be made. Jean Rhys is concerned with women, especially with women who are on the fringes of society, and she looks in detail at their economic and class situation. The innate, or incipient, feminism of her work stood out more clearly if we read her alongside the works of literary Bloomsbury: Virginia Woolf, E. M. Forster or even T. S. Eliot. The woman supine in a boat on the Thames in Eliot's *The Waste Land* was no doubt a Rhys heroine, taking for herself, as Petronella does, something positive out of the world to keep her going through the next bad patch. Both pieces identify the shallowness of that existence, but Rhys gives us a wider view, one of the woman dependent on dreams to counter her depression. Virginia Woolf's work is an illuminating comparison, as she often wrote about the ennui and depression afflicting women of the upper and middle classes. Jean Rhys, for all the surface depression of her story, does show women who are able to adapt and change and ultimately survive on their own account. That is no small strength, and one that feminism should recognise and acknowledge.

Our second story was 'Advancing Luna and Ida B. Wells', by Alice Walker from *You Can't Keep a Good Woman Down* (Women's

Press, 1982.) The first-person narrator recalls 1965 and the campaigns for civil rights and the registration of Black voters in the
American South. It seems directly autobiographical. The narrator
and Luna have both come in from outside to help, but whereas the
narrator is Black, and accepted by and easy with the people they
have come to help register and vote, Luna is white. They become
friends and later live together. Much later, Luna reveals that she
had been raped, while in the South, by a fellow activist, a Black
man (Freddie Pye). The story concerns both the two women's
friendship and their involvement in the civil rights campaign, as
well as with the way to write it. The author struggles with the
weight of understanding rape, the contradictions it brings up for
her and the pressure of history at her back, when Black men were
lynched for the 'crime' of looking at white women while the rape
of Black women by white men was condoned.

We had these questions for the group reading 'Advancing Luna':

1 How does the author, if she does, write about love, sex and
   friendship?
2 What is the context of this story?
3 How does it compare with the other writing we've considered?
4 How would you describe the style of the story?
5 In this particular context, rape cannot be seen only as an act of
   violence against women. What is your reaction to this?
6 Can love, sex and friendship be seen in political terms? Must
   they be seen in these terms? How does Alice Walker treat these
   matters?

Discussion took place over a couple of weeks and we spent time
both discussing our responses to the story and the guiding questions
and deciding how best to introduce it to the other group.

We found it a very difficult and challenging story both to read
and to discuss. The story does not offer a single interpretation of
the events it recounts. The reader is thoroughly disturbed, unable
to settle at one point in the story, to identify with one character
and read the events from their point of view. The notes at the end,
which are headed 'Afterwords', 'Afterwards', 'Second Thoughts',
and also include discarded notes and a section entitled 'Imaginary
Knowledge' and a postscript written in Havana, Cuba in 1976, all
expand upon the dilemmas for the writer about how to tell the
story. These are as important as the story itself, and the reader is
forced to move between them, as she is forced to move backwards

and forwards between the issues of race and gender, to ask who are the victims, who are the perpetrators?

What is made clear, too, is that the issue is not just a writerly one to the extent that it is solely about what happens on the page, or how best to express words, thoughts or ideas. It is the consequences of those words that stop Alice Walker's pen, and moves it in different, sometimes contradictory directions. The concern with the political consequences of her actions as a writer mirror and expand the concerns of the story which are with the consequences of action, and the difficult issue of taking responsibility for our own actions, as well as exploring the question of can we, or should we, ever try to take responsibility for other people's actions?

The story was centred, for us, in friendship. At the outset, Luna and Alice both understand the personal as a universal term, they believe in the ability and right of friendship to cross all boundaries and see no problems in friendships across lines of race and class. Gradually, this is revealed to be a partial truth, a worthy ideal but one which is far from realisation. It is also, in the context of friendship between women, made clear that the pressures on these women, and the conditions for equal, loving behaviour between them, is determined from outside. The women's issue is also a race issue, and a class issue. In Alice Walker's Imaginary Ending, Freddie Pye calls up Luna when he is stranded in Brooklyn. He has been brought up by 'The Movement' to address a meeting. He is on display as

> an example of what 'the system' did to 'the little people' in the South. They asked him to tell about the thirty-seven times he had been jailed. The thirty-five times he had been beaten . . . He knew the rich people and his own leaders perceived he was nothing: a broken man, unschooled, unskilled at anything.
>
> (Walker 1984: 101)

At the end of the meeting, everyone leaves. There have been no arrangements made for Freddie and, remembering Luna, he looks up her number in the phone book. Alice Walker then describes a scene in which Luna feeds him and allows him to stay the night, but locks her own door and takes a knife to bed with her. In the early hours, kept awake by worrying whether Freddie is uncomfortable, she goes to him, says he can come into the bed but shows him the knife. During that night, they talk. Freddie speaks first, about his life, Luna about whether she had the right to scream when Freddie was raping her. Alice Walker, in her commentary, then says:

> Two people have now become 'characters'. I have forced them to talk until they reached the stumbling block of the rape, *which they must remove themselves*, before proceeding to a place from which it will be possible to insist on a society in which Luna's word alone on rape can never be used to intimidate an entire people, and in which an innocent black man's protestation of innocence of rape is unprejudicially heard. Until such a society is created, relationships of affection between black men and white women will always be poisoned – from within as from without – by historical fear and the threat of violence, and solidarity among black and white women is only rarely likely to exist.
>
> (Walker 1984: 102)

There was a long discussion to locate what exactly was the context for this story. We felt that it was race and gender, and began by seeing a conflict between them until we realised that it was only because we were white women that we could make that separation: for Black women, the issue is always race and gender. Whereas we could stand outside that conflict, they live it, day by day. To understand the story, we had to find a way of dealing with the race issue. We had to try and bracket ourselves out, in order to understand how these issues were being experienced and articulated by a Black woman. We had then to read the story as white women too, to see ourselves as agents, rather than victims, of oppression. We had all thought about rape in relation to women before. Some women had quite sophisticated understandings of how rape as an act of violence against women controls and restricts women's freedom. What was new, and difficult for us to see, was how in Walker's story the effect of rape on a woman is made less significant than the political struggle over race and civil rights.

It is Luna herself who makes that decision. It is much later that she tells Alice, and only Alice, what happened and in reply to her question 'What did you do?' replies that she did nothing that required making a noise. Alice's response is the split response, the imperative to hold two quite opposite courses of action in her head at once, so that the story slowly unfolds to us as the reality of Black women's lives:

> 'Why didn't you scream?' I felt I would have screamed my head off.
> 'You know why.'
> I did. I had seen a photograph of Emmett Till's body just after it was pulled from the river. I had seen photographs of white folks standing in a circle roasting something that had talked to them in their own language before they tore out its tongue. I knew why, all right.

> (Walker 1984: 92)

There are no details given about the rape; it is treated impersonally. The detail, and the struggling towards the conclusion that there are no clear-cut answers, is focused upon the consequences of the rape, and Luna's silence, for the Black struggle. Alice Walker, however, isn't just letting go of Luna. Throughout the story she is presented in complimentary terms as a woman of courage and integrity, but she is always presented from Alice's viewpoint. Luna does not speak for herself, thus occupying the position so familiar to Black women, indeed Black people, in our narratives that we rarely remark upon it. As our group members struggled with the difficult emotions this raised for us, it became clear that we needed to know more about the history of race in America to fully understand the story. British history had its own particular shameful past where race is concerned, and there, too, the supposed threat to white women from Black men has been exploited. However, the particular history of the South: the lynching of Black men, the real power white women had over those men and the exploitation of that by white men on the one hand, and the defence and protection of Black men by Black women on the other, was something quite distinct. We wondered whether we could ever really understand how that history had shaped the consciousness and memory of the people, Black and white, born into it.

In discussion, though, we realised that even if that particular history was something we did not know or share, we had experienced something similar. We talked about the conflicts over the 'Reclaim the Night' marches in the late 1970s and early 1980s. Outside London, many marches went through inner city areas with large Black populations. A number of Black women refused to participate in the protests, arguing that women were confirming stereotypes of Black men as criminal and more likely to assault and rape them. Equally, there have been tensions within feminism between certain forms of separatism and women whose allegiance, and protection, lies within a wider community or politics defined by race or class. The issue here was by no means clear-cut.

We went on to talk about the ways in which certain forms of political struggle and solidarity demanded sexual favours of women almost as a mark of their political allegiance. In these cases the coercion can be either subtle or violent, but it is still sex by coercive means. One woman told us that when she was a teenage member of a left-wing organisation, there were assumptions about sexual availability that had been jokingly referred to as 'the horizontal road to socialism'. To refuse sex was seen as reactionary and bourgeois. Women were familiar with situations that had arisen during the 1984 miners' strike, when there was the expectation of sex from male miners on fund-raising tours.

Although we talked and argued about Walker's story for a long time, and were trying to come to terms with our own racism, all of us found that our empathy was with the raped woman. Although it made us feel ashamed to say it, we admitted to feeling angry at the way she was treated and were most shocked by Alice's reaction to being told:

> Suddenly I was embarrassed. Then angry. Very, very angry. *How dare she tell me this!* I thought.
>
> (Walker 1984: 93)

Somehow, having that empathy with Luna made it possible to appreciate the enormity of the gulf between white and Black women's experience of the world. Although we could not think as Alice did, it seemed very important to be clear that we could not, to acknowledge just how different our lives, emotions and political priorities were. The struggle we had with our feelings and our thoughts did help us to understand those that Alice herself was going through to the extent of making it clear that we did not and could not empathise. Reaching this conclusion wasn't about an easy retreat into our separate worlds, it was more a recognition of the conditions under which we strive for justice, and friendship, between races.

The style in which the story is written excited us. We had never come across such an impersonal, reflective style of writing before and we were impressed by the way in which Walker had found the courage to treat such difficult and emotive subjects with a control and distance that didn't deny or diminish their emotional power. It seemed to us, too, to be a piece of writing that exposed and questioned the normal conventions of writing in a way that extended our understanding of the process. The title itself, 'Advancing Luna and Ida B. Wells', gave us one insight. 'Advancing' we understood to mean moving on, and the story's successive drafts and redrafts underlined how, with this set of issues and with this particular social and political conjunction, there could only ever be moving on. There would be no arrival, no end point and final judgements. The title reference to Ida B. Wells indicates that Luna's story must be understood with reference to everything that she fought for and represents. The one cannot be advanced without the other, and Ida B. Wells is a touchstone for Alice Walker, her conscience and her oracle. Many of us did not know who she was and we found out.

She was born a few months before emancipation and worked first as a teacher and later as a journalist. In 1892 she launched an anti-lynching crusade, initially through *Free Speech*, the newspaper she worked for, an action that cost her her job and forced her to leave Memphis, Tennessee. She made speaking tours throughout the northern states of America and in Britain to promote her cause; she also published pamphlets. She took petitions to the President and worked in the National Association for the Advancement of Coloured People. Her position on the lynchings was clear, as her own writings show. The editorial in *Free Speech*, which caused the paper to be closed, was written in response to eight lynchings.

Alice Walker, exercised by how to write about rape, turns to Ida B. Wells for clarification and strength:

> I read Ida B. Wells's autobiography three times, as a means of praying to her spirit to forgive me. My prayer, as I turned the pages, went like this: *'Please forgive me. I am a writer.'*
>
> (Walker 1984: 93)

In the dialogue she sets down between them, Alice is shown refusing to take the advice – the imperative – that Ida B. Wells gives:

> *Write nothing. Nothing at all. It will be used against black men and therefore against all of us . . . No matter what you think you know, no matter what you feel about it, say nothing. And to your dying*

breath. Which, to my mind, is virtually useless advice to give to a writer.

(Walker 1984: 94)

Reading 'Advancing Luna' was a powerfully educative and politicising process for us. We had been made aware of how much we didn't know about Black American history, and in dwelling on that we realised, too, how little we understood or knew about our country's past from a Black perspective. The story had forced us to consider the Black woman's point of view:

> *Who knows what the black woman thinks of rape? Who has asked her? Who cares?* Who has even properly acknowledged that she and not the white woman in this story is the most likely victim of rape?

(Walker 1984: 93)

and to look from her side at the problem of inter-racial women's friendships. In order to do so, it has to problematise, rather than suggest or permit, any kind of resolution to the dilemmas it articulates.

3

DIFFERENCES

In the early 1980s a Black woman was appointed in London as an advisory teacher on Women's Studies. Part of her job involved visiting Adult Education Institutes and talking with women teachers who were involved in Women's Studies courses. She was eagerly welcomed; the Women's Studies course is often thought to be a very poor relation to mainstream classes, and the teachers involved can experience isolation and disparagement from their colleagues. But one question kept coming up from the women the advisory teacher met: 'Why do you keep talking about race?'

Thus do we all deny the complexities and differences that make up our own and other women's lives. The title 'Women's Studies' (as women's movement) suggests an idea of 'women' that applies across the board, but as feminists we can no longer accept this. Race, ethnicity, class, sexuality, language, age and disability are all essential and integral parts of women's experience that beg the question of a homogeneity of sisterhood and demand consideration. Organisers of Women's Studies courses must incorporate the struggles against prejudice and discrimination into their thinking and planning; analyses of those prejudices, and of the ways in which society has denied and ignored them, are essential to curriculum development. Within the specific area of women's writing, tutors must expand their own consciousnesses of the racism, classism and heterosexism in writing by white women, and in the academic traditions of Britain and North America.

Power operates to subdue difference by ignoring it. We know from our analysis of sexism that ignoring what is 'different' is a highly effective means of silencing it; by pretending, consciously or otherwise, that the different does not exist, we quickly create conditions in which it actually ceases to exist, or is so repressed as to be invisible. Patriarchy has systematically ignored, and often silenced, women's creativity, and women have had to struggle long and painfully to reclaim themselves and their work. But power operates through a hierarchy of privileges; amongst women this leads to the establishment of oppositions around oppression that threaten our solidarity and common cause. These oppositions, around race, class, sexuality, age, must be recognised and challenged before women can achieve any sense of joint power.

For white women, for heterosexual women, for middle-class women, the first step in challenging male oppression is to recognise their own built-in privilege and power by virtue of their whiteness, their sexuality, their class. And the best way to achieve such awareness is to listen to, to read the words of, Black women, lesbians, working-class women. The analyses, painfully and carefully worked out by these women, of racism, heterosexism, and classism, are important not only in terms of evaluating and questioning our own behaviour as oppressors, but also as wider critiques of our whole society. Above all, they make essential connections between the forces of oppression and the ways in which they operate the divide-and-rule principle. Every time we write the list – race, sexuality, class, age, etc., etc. – we are aware that we are simplifying matters, separating out again into various -isms what are, in fact, complex and inter-related experiences.

One approach towards an unravelling of these complex issues is a consideration of difference, whether in terms of race, class, sexuality, alone or in any combination. In her essay 'Age, Race, Class and Sex: Women Redefining Difference' (published in *Sister Outsider*, 1984) Audre Lorde pinpoints difference and the failure to acknowledge it as 'the most serious threat to the mobilization of joint power'. The notion of difference posits a norm in which power resides; those outside the norm may often identify one difference and hang all their oppression on that, losing sight of the connections between oppressions, and of the fact that they may themselves practise other oppressions, if only by omission.

Acknowledging differences between women, analysing and understanding their implications, and changing one's practice to challenge oppression may seem dangerous and painful. The advisory teacher who was asked why she kept bringing race into courses in Women's Studies took risks, and women teaching from their own feminism and experience must also be risk-takers. It is essential that women discover ways to reunify, to break through the bland and betraying concepts of unexamined 'sisterhood' into a true unity and strength.

RACISM

Racism pervades Women's Studies courses, as it does the women's movement and all of British society. The aims of Women's Studies courses have to include an understanding of the nature of racism, and a positive anti-racist stance to challenge it.

Although there are now some Black women teachers for Women's Studies courses, the majority are still white, and often middle class: it is their responsibility to take on racism within their own attitudes and within the curriculum. A few years ago it was not uncommon to hear white teachers at education conferences saying, 'I don't have a problem with racism – I don't have any Black students', or even, 'I don't have a problem with racism – the Black students fit in well with the others.' This position, never tenable, reflects a deep-seated failure to recognise the per-vasive nature of racism within our society; moreover, it plays the familiar game of blaming the victim, suggesting that rac-ism is only a problem for Black people. It reveals the invidious nature of an education system that presents the success story of a small island managing to gain control of the seas and large parts of the earth – without mentioning that success was only obtained through the enslavement and exploitation of millions of people, justified, whether they were African, Indian, Irish or Chinese, on the grounds of their inherent inferiority to the white master-race.

Such attitudes are still reflected in the activities of the Conserva-tive government both abroad (the Falklands war, the bombing of Tripoli, recalcitrance over nuclear de-escalation), and at home through a series of Acts of Parliament that have empowered the state in its determination to consolidate the white, male middle-class entrepreneurial power-base, and to disenfranchise and deny rights to those who are poor, Black, lesbian or gay, working-class, or any combination of these.

The pressures brought about by these 'reforms' – and it would be foolish to deny their force – operate to extinguish solidarity between oppressed groups. Tories also argue against radical educa-tion, and it is within this context that Women's Studies courses may find themselves having to justify their existence. It is, therefore, essential that Women's Studies tutors are able to present a sustained and pro-active stance that incorporates an awareness of the needs of all women, and recognises that those needs may be different and diverse.

Black women in Britain, Africa, the Middle East, Asia and America have considered, analysed and described the nature of racism as it particularly affects the women's movement, and it is to their work that we must ultimately turn. But initially we should examine writing by white women to attempt to trace the ways in which the women's movement itself became both a perpetrator and a victim of racism. The remainder of this section will deal with writing by Black and white women, and will include short descriptions of relevant texts and suggestions for their use.

For white women, who have identified themselves as oppressed and have been through the painful processes of learning what that oppression has done to them, there is often a reluctance to accept that they still retain the ability to oppress others. But oppressions are not separate and clear-cut, and it is in the nature of oppression to operate on different levels and in different ways. It is sometimes too easy for white women to assume that the experience of sexism is equal and undifferentiated, to identify a common enemy, and expect all women to unite in solidarity against that enemy. And when, instead of solidarity, white women find themselves challenged by Black women on their racism, there has been a tendency to defensiveness, to retreat in hurt and guilty silence, to talk about 'splitting the movement' and generally to exhibit symptoms of paralysis, which may easily be seen as inertia, as a refusal to hear and to act.

There is a small body of writing by white women that has begun the long struggle against racism. For example, Adrienne Rich's essay 'Disloyal to Civilisation: Feminism, Racism, Gynephobia' (published in *On Lies, Secrets and Silences*, 1980) sets out the complex and sometimes destructive connection between the histories of Black and white women in America, and the relationship between feminism and racism. It is a painfully written essay, painful to read, and acknowledges, among much else, just how deeply embedded in white women is racism and the images it creates of both Black and white women. This is an essential point, for racism is about definition, and in defining Black people, men and women, it also defines white people – and the image of white women implicitly included in racist theory is precisely that image challenged by feminists: mothering, submissive, dependent. This point is taken up and expanded by Marilyn Frye in her essay 'On Being White' (1983, reprinted in *Trouble and Strife* 4, Winter 1984). She describes, too, the ways in which White women have rendered Black women invisible and powerless through ignorance of Black women's lives, histories and issues, and posits White supremacy as something with which white women collude unless they clearly choose to disaffiliate themselves and support the anti-racist struggle.

Both Rich and Frye consider the paralysing effect of guilt arising from white women's recognition of their own collusion in racism; Janet Martens and Ruth Frankenberg in their paper 'White Racism: More Than a Moral Issue' (*Trouble and Strife* 5, Spring 1985) suggest ways of moving forward through anti-racist feminist analysis to ultimate coalition, with white and Black women working side by side in the diverse struggles against patriarchy.

The most significant effect of these essays for white women is to focus on their own racism and how it operates; that is, to remove the burden and responsibility for racism away from its victims and on to its perpetrators. We should all examine and question our own learning experience constantly, and not be afraid to acknowledge errors and find their source.

Two recent examples from our own experience come to mind, where the assumptions of white women tutors created situations in which Black women were forced to point up differences between their experience and our own. In the first instance, a group of Return to Study students were in the introductory session of a short course in Women's Studies. The group consisted of eight women students, four of whom were Black (three Afro-Caribbean, ranging in age from mid-twenties to sixties, and one Somali woman, in her early thirties), and four were white working-class, in their early twenties. There were three white middle-class tutors, in their mid to late thirties. As a preliminary exercise, the tutors had chosen to look at women's magazines to consider the images they present of women and what pressures they bring to bear on us, and then to think back to our teenage years and to recall what images and pressures had operated then to affect our own self-images.

The exercise worked well, with all the women noting the absence of Black women and working women in the magazine, and commenting freely on how relevant or otherwise such publications were to them. But when we came to consider our own pasts and adolescent experiences we encountered enormous diversities and differences – which we, the tutors, had not anticipated and thus subsequently failed to provide an adequate response. For example, the older Afro-Caribbean woman had left school at nine, had lived with her aunt and her grandmother, and had begun to work in the fields as soon as she left school. She had grown up in a rural culture before the Second World War, and had consequently little experience of the films, television and popular music that most of us were recounting.

At the same time, she emphasised the happiness and security of her childhood; her main regret was interrupted education, but to some extent she substituted for that the wealth of natural beauty in the countryside and the religious certainty in her home. It was impossible, however, to sustain a dialogue about her experience because we were so ignorant of it; we could ask questions, but could not but make her feel that her experience was unusual and extraordinary because our own, and that of the other white women in the group, was seen to be the norm.

An even more extreme example came from our reactions to the Somali woman in the group. She was married at the age of eleven, and had her first child at thirteen. Her attendance at the classes had always been erratic, largely because of the demands of a family of nine, regular illness, and a husband who expected her to wait on him in the tradition of the good Muslim wife. Her straightforward recitation of the facts of her teenage years contrasted sharply with our white, flippant, jokes about boyfriends and pop stars, and again the disparity between our experiences set against our implied assumptions of common ground created uneasiness and unequal demands for her to elaborate on her differences from us.

What follows here indicates the ways in which good intentions can often prevent the tutor from understanding her own assumptions and prejudices. *The Heart of the Race* (Bryan, Dadzie, Scafe 1985) was published by Virago, and was the first full-length documentation of Black women's lives in Britain to be written by Black women who live in Britain. The introduction, 'The Ties That Bind', is a clear, unemotional account of Britain's implication in slavery and imperialism, and firmly places Britain's industrial wealth and prosperity on the bodies of slaves:

> A local writer said of Bristol at the time 'there is not a brick
> in that city but what is cemented with the blood of slaves'.
> (Bryan, Dadzie, Scafe 1985: 7)

As white tutors we eagerly grabbed this book to use in our teaching, partly to inform students of its existence and partly to use the word of Black women rather than White people in presenting aspects of Black history. However, we made serious misjudgements both in the way we presented the material, and in its effects on the group.

The group in question was a mixed Black and white literacy group, who had been looking at history and writing. It is usual in mixed ability literacy groups, where students have varying reading skills, to simplify material, and this was done by the white tutor. Given the source of this material, we asked a Black tutor to look at the simplification, and it was slightly amended at this stage. The original version of the piece was also available to the students, but most of them would not have been able to read it without considerable help.

As we read the piece together, it was clearly causing considerable pain to some of the Black students. The pain and anger arose because the Black women concerned had only recently discovered for themselves the full history of slavery and could hardly bear to consider it. White women in the group also felt shocked and helpless in the face of what, for some of them, was new, or newly perceived, knowledge: one White woman recounted her experience of learning about the Middle Passage as part of geography lessons, reducing the human and political aspects of slavery to a matter of trade routes. Only later did she fully realise that the cargo carried on this route had been human.

In addition, some of the Black women were Afro-Caribbean while others were from Nigeria, Kenya and Aden; discovering shared, if different, experiences of colonialisation and imperialism became a significant factor in cementing relationships between the Black women. They questioned the usefulness (perhaps manipulation would be a better word) of white tutors who created a situation which produced such pain and anger, but provided no indication of where the anger could or should be directed, pointing out that at this particular time (just after the Handsworth riots) it was no wonder Black people were rising on the streets.

67

Finally, the Black women criticised the tutor for exposing the white women in the group both to a painful awareness of their own guilty history, and to the anger of the inheritors of that history.

It is essential to analyse what went wrong in situations like this, and where the tutor fell into racist assumptions. Thanks to the considerable generosity of the Black women in this group we were able to recognise two major points on which to act:

1 The assumption that history and information is equally available and therefore known to everyone. White history, whether taught in Britain, the Caribbean or former colonial states of Africa and Asia, is history from the white viewpoint and is invariably presented as the truth. The power and ability to challenge and rewrite that history has to be acquired and learned – it is not freely given. The same applies to writing – we should never forget that access to non-mainstream literature depends on economic power, and the cultural skills that we as tutors should be teaching, not assuming are already present. Moreover, we cannot view such hidden and distorted histories with an objective, academic eye. These histories are hidden precisely because they are shameful and can empower their victims; to present them neutrally is to deny the righteous anger and pain of the oppressed, and the implication and guilt of the oppressor.

2 We need to be very careful about manipulating strong emotions of anger and pain, and to think clearly about why we create situations which will raise them and how they are to be used. The students' criticism, of stirring up anger as an end in itself (even unintentionally) without suggesting ways in which that anger can be used, was right.

These examples may seem extreme; more important perhaps are the smaller, daily examples of assumptions and prejudice that we, as white tutors, fail to notice, and Black women are too weary and despairing to pick us up on. And the reason we fail to notice them brings us back to the issue of differences, which we all too often also fail to notice, or we evade it through our ignorance.

It is the question of differences that is crucial to our understanding both of the way in which white women operate as racists and of the way forward. In her essay 'Age, Race, Class and Sex'

Audre Lorde succinctly and devastatingly outlines the differences that exist in patriarchal society, and how by ignoring them we can never create a truly unified movement for the liberation of women.

Certainly there are very real differences between us of race, age and sex. But it is not those differences between us that are separating us. It is rather our refusal to recognise those differences, and to examine the distortions which result from our misnaming them and their effects upon human behaviour and expectation . . . to extract these distortions from our living at the same time as we recognise, reclaim, and define those differences upon which they are imposed . . . I believe one of the reasons white women have such difficulty reading Black women's work is because of their reluctance to see Black women as women and different from themselves . . .

(Lorde 1984: 115–21)

Much of the fiction by Black writers in America is set firmly in, and often centres on, the Black community and concerns itself with both male–female relationships, and family relationships, within that community (e.g. the writing of Alice Walker, Toni Morrison, Zora Neale Hurston, Toni Cade Bambara, Gloria Naylor, Paule Marshall and others). By comparison, Black African and Afro-Caribbean women writing in Britain often place their characters in the white community, whether in society at large (for example Joan Riley, Jackie Kay, Buchi Emecheta) or in more women-centred situations (for example Barbara Burford). Writers in Britain also depict life 'at home', in the Caribbean, in Africa, or in the Indian subcontinent, considering the transition from colonial life to Britain, with all its tensions, false expectations and disillusions (e.g. Merle Collins, Grace Nichols, Buchi Emecheta, Jean Breeze). These writers, in America and in Britain, are deeply concerned with racism and its effects, and this runs as a constant subtext throughout their writing. But it is not the only theme, and it is essential for white readers to grasp the many and various ways in which racism operates and to recognise its constant presence, while simultaneously reading for other themes, other concerns.

For Asian women, the experience of living in Britain reflects that of African and Afro-Caribbean women to the extent that it represents non-white women living within a white society, but it is often strongly rooted in specific domestic and cultural backgrounds. But the struggle is against a racist and culturally exclusive society. For example, Ravinder Randhawa's *A Wicked Old Woman* (Women's Press 1987) presents, through flashbacks and contemporary narratives, the strength of family ties (to the point of suffocation sometimes); how these ties can provide support for the family against racism, but how they may need to be subverted for women to find independence. The same pattern can be found in stories in *Right of Way*, an anthology of stories and poems from the Asian Women Writers Workshop (Women's Press 1988). The anthology presents stories concerned with the often uneasy connections between Asians and Afro-Caribbeans, for example, *Leaving Home* by Rahil Gupta.

There is also a strong strain of writing about life in the Indian subcontinent, both remembered and visited: 'A Day for Nuggo', by Rukhsan Ahmad, for instance, considers both class and gender divisions and their effects on one poor working woman, while Leena Dhingra's 'The Debt' exposes the naivety of Anjali returning to India for the first time on her own, as a working woman. Many Asian writers use their own cultural styles in new and exciting ways to depict situations of women in alien societies: Suniti Namjoshi (*Conversations with Cow, Feminist Fables, Because of India*) and Maxine Hong Kingston (*The Woman Warrior* and *China Men*) are examples.

The reasons for the varying contexts of Black writing are historical, and relevant to the ways in which readers will react to the text. In North America, Black people have been present, though often invisible, for 200 years. The histories of slavery and abolition, of southern and northern cultures, of discrimination and oppression, of lynching and rape, of poverty and civil rights, run like an underground stream beneath the broad highway of American aggrandisement and increasing world domination. As such there is a tradition within American writing that includes the depiction and stereotyped characterisation of Black people which can be traced back to and beyond Harriet Beecher Stowe. (The depiction and characterisation of Native Americans also reflect stereotyped 'European' views, such as the 'Noble Savage' and involved the almost complete suppression of indigenous cultures. The revival of these cultures has only recently begun to express itself in written form, which we have not considered here.) Occasionally, very occasionally, a white writer like Eudora Welty has attempted to tackle racism head-on. In addition, Black writers have their own traditions, not always accessible or acceptable (for example, writing in the vernacular) and often extinguished prematurely. Writers such as Zora Neale Hurston, Lorraine Hansberry and Ann Petry work from within frameworks of support and recognised attitudes, and often against stereotyped images.

Zora Neale Hurston's Jamie in *Their Eyes were Watching God*, has been brought up in the belief that the Black woman is 'the mule of the world'. Forced to marry an older man who beats her, she escapes from that marriage into another with an ambitious man who wants her to be decorative and a credit to himself, and finally she elopes with a no-good gambler who treats her as an equal. She is, therefore, in constant revolt against male domination and a world in which roles for Black women are firmly delineated and curtailed. She refuses passivity, refuses convention and fate, and ends up alone but with a sense of fulfilment. In this she is not unlike Sula, in Toni Morrison's 1973 eponymous novel. Independence, toughness, singlemindedness and something amounting almost to irresponsibility characterise the Black women who attempt to force their way in a world both internally and externally policed by those who would maintain the Black woman's place at the bottom of the heap.

The history of the suppression of Black women both as independent champions of Black people and as creators of Black culture is too often subsumed in the general history of Black people in America. Harriet Tubman, Sojourner Truth and Ida B. Wells are the better-known (but still not enough known) of the women who subverted the deathly powers of slavery, fought for emancipation and enfranchisement, and waged bitter struggles against lynching and the vicious racist stereotyping that endorsed it. The theme of the Black woman as suppressed artist can be found in the writing of Alice Walker. The essay 'In Search of Our Mothers' Gardens' postulates Black women's creativity, suppressed in terms of formal expression, following whatever channels do remain open: gardening, quilting, cooking, raising children, thus not only retaining and passing on an undiminished sense of beauty and life, but also reaching back to a common African past where what was valued was precisely the celebration of the everyday:

And perhaps in Africa over two hundred years ago there was just such a mother; perhaps she painted vivid and daring decorations in oranges and yellows and greens on the walls of her hut; perhaps she sang – in a voice like Roberta Flack's – sweetly over the compounds of her village; perhaps she wove the most stunning mats or told the most ingenious stories of all the village storytellers. Perhaps she was herself a poet – though only her daughter's name is signed to the poems that we know.

(Walker 1984: 243)

This theme forms the core of the story 'Everyday Use'. The first-person narrator is the mother of two daughters, Maggie, disabled in a fire and remaining quietly at home with her mother in the country, and Dee, ambitious and sophisticated, who lives in the city, and is paying a visit to her mother and sister. She arrives with her man, insisting that they are both addressed by the new African names they have assumed, and begins at once to disparage the rural backwardness of her sister, while exclaiming over the ageing and well-used furniture and implements in the house. She wants to take away the churn top as a decoration for her own home, and then starts rummaging through the quilts, made and remade by the women of the family through several generations. Again she desires them, not to use, but to hang as decorations. But her mother refuses, for the quilts are for Maggie when she marries. Dee flounces out:

'You just don't understand', she said, as Maggie and I came out to the car.
'What don't I understand?' I wanted to know.
'Your heritage', she said.

(Walker 1984: 59)

The story illustrates the conflict between the Roots movement, with its tendency to petrify everyday items into moribund art forms, and the forces of creativity that these forms often represent. Dee has rejected the oppressor's culture by her espousal of African culture, but she fails to recognise the life force that persists despite and in opposition to that culture, and which appears in the everyday objects created by hard work and determination and intended for use until worn out – when new ones would be made following the age-old patterns. This continuity of objects is also a continuity of persons, who live on and are remembered in the artefacts they created and in the skills they passed on – by which message the story comes full circle, for this is also part of the old tradition, the African tradition that Dee has adopted without becoming fully part of.

Conflict is a constantly recurring theme, between rural and urban life (see also Maya Angelou's *I Know Why the Caged Bird Sings*), between generations (see the dialogue between the mother and her terribly aware and sophisticated children in Toni Cade Bambara's 'My Man Bovanne'), and between women and men (see Jamie's relationship with Joe Starks in Zora Neale Hurston's *Their Eyes Were Watching God*, and the husband and wife in Alice Walker's 'Coming Apart').

Beyond conflict there lies reconciliation and where this occurs, or is hinted at, it is primarily between women. Three novels, Paule Marshall's *Brown Girl, Brownstones*, Toni Morrison's *Sula*, and Alice Walker's *The Color Purple*, may be taken as examples. Each book is firmly based in a Black community with few, if any, white characters. But the struggle for survival of the Black people, and especially of the women, reflects their situation as the lowest, least economically powerful class in society. Families form the context of the novels, each of which is set in the past.

Sula describes the lives of the Peace family in a small Ohio town between 1919 and 1965, particularly the lives of three generations of women, Eva, Hannah and Sula, and of Sula's girlfriend, Nel. One of the questions that echoes throughout the novel, and many others, is Hannah's to her mother, Eva: 'Mamma, did you ever love us?' (Morrison 1982: 65), for what is often lost in the soul-destroying struggle to survive against dulling poverty and a hostile society is precisely the ability, the energy, to provide affection.

This need for her mother's affection and approval in conflict with her own need for independence pervades Selina's relationship with Silla in *Brown Girl, Brownstones*, set in New York during and after the Second World War, and telling the story of the Deighton family, the parents Barbadian immigrants, one of the proud minorities within the American Black community. Silla works long hours, first as a domestic help and later in factories, both to support her family and to realise her ambition of moving to their own house in a better area. Her ambition contrasts starkly with her husband Deighton's easygoing optimism and fecklessness, with his dreams of returning to Barbados; she comes to represent a harsh, cold force of rectitude and repression to Selina, while Deighton seems to embody sunshine and laughter, but ultimate inertia.

For most of the book Selina is locked in an unremitting battle with her mother who is referred to, chillingly, as 'the mother', but in the end it is Silla whom she acknowledges as the model for her own life:

> 'Everybody used to call me Deighton's Selina but they were wrong, because you see I'm truly your child. Remember how you used to talk about how you left home and came here alone as a girl of eighteen and was your own woman? I used to love hearing that. And that's what I want. I want it!
>
> (Marshall 1959: 307)

The struggle for independence forms part of another theme common to these books: the conflict between the support of the family and community and the need to break away from it, if only temporarily. Independence often brings loneliness and isolation; it can also mean severing the bonds of marriage as well as those of family.

Women leaving and returning is a theme that runs through much Black American women's writing: they go to the south, to the north, to the Caribbean, to Africa. And there exists also a sense of the past in which women were strong and powerful and passed on knowledge and wisdom. It is there in the kitchen talk of Silla Boyce's friends in *Brown Girl, Brownstones*; it pervades Nettie's letters from Africa to her sister Celie in *The Color Purple*. Beyond these specific novels, it informs the poetry of Audre Lorde, particularly in *The Black Unicorn* (1978), and creates a link between American and British Black writing in the consciousness of an African past that, despite the differing experiences since, is vital and precious to all displaced Black women.

This link can be observed through a sample of poems by Audre Lorde, Grace Nichols and Iyamide Hazeley. We suggest three poems which can be used in a comparative study: '125th Street and Abomey' by Audre Lorde; 'Waterpot' by Grace Nichols and 'When you have Emptied our Calabashes' by Iyamide Hazeley. The poems trace back from contemporary North America or Britain through slavery and the plantations of the south or of the Caribbean to West Africa, and the line of descent is matrilineal. Sometimes, for Lorde and Nichols, the experience reflects the terrors of seizure, of the Middle Passage and enslavement; sometimes it is the brutalising humiliation and depredation of colonialism. At all times, Black women are recapturing and energising themselves with the ancient strengths and dignities of their race that were trampled but not destroyed by the white European oppressors.

Although the poems track back, there is no nostalgia here, but instead a sustaining and forceful awareness of a long struggle not yet won. And it is reflected in the international perspective of Black women who identify closely with the struggles of their sisters all over the world. This identification has, for example, been focused on Winnie Mandela, but has also involved women of Palestine, Nicaragua, the Philippines, Iran, India and any place where women are fighting for freedom and against racism. The journal *Outwrite* provided a forum for the international view, which many white women have failed to encompass.

This failure reflects, especially in Britain, simultaneously a narrow and blinkered world view and the sense of superior isolation that so affects the history of Black people in Britain. Although there have always been some Black people in Britain, it is only in the last forty years that Black communities have established themselves in the country. Prior to that, Britain's Black slaves, colonial subjects and eventually citizens were kept firmly at a distance, in Africa, in Asia, in India and in the Caribbean. British white supremacy, however, pervaded every aspect of their lives, imposing laws, religion, education, and restricting trade and development. Indigenous cultures and languages, traditional customs and morals, locally developed politics and economics were ruthlessly destroyed as being primitive, ignorant and heathen. The rule of white supremacist Britain, its justifications and rectitude, was deeply inculcated in the minds of white people as the natural order of things. It is this ingrained racism with its multiplicity of distortions and hypocrisies, that we must endeavour to eradicate.

One noticeable effect of racism in Britain is the lack of published work by Black women, especially when compared with America. A significant factor is the lack of accessibility to publishing. This, combined with an educational system that has only recently begun even to consider the issues of language for second language and Black British students, has effectively excluded Black writers from both a cultural identity and a public. Very slowly, Black women are now beginning to be published, and this is largely due to small presses such as Sheba. Producing maybe half a dozen titles a year, with little capital, Sheba introduced British readers to Audre Lorde when they published *Zami* in 1982, and provided a platform for

British Black writers like Jackie Kay, Barbara Burford and Rashida Khan in *Everyday Matters* 2 and *A Dangerous Knowing*, the first collection of poetry by Black women, published in about 1984.

Since 1983 *Spare Rib* magazine has also consistently published creative writing, polemic and interviews with Black women writers. The Women's Press has, over the last few years, provided an outlet for Black women's writing from America, Africa, Turkey, India, China, Japan, Iran, Syria, Lebanon and Palestine.

To date, only a small proportion of this writing is by writers living in Britain: *The Unbelonging*, *Waiting in the Twilight* and *Romance* by Joan Riley; *Angel* by Merle Collins; *A Wicked Old Woman* by Ravinder Randhawa; the collection *Watchers and Seekers*, and autobiographical writing like *In My Own Name* by Sharan-Jeet Shan. Virago, the largest and most well-established of the women's presses, has published little Black writing – Grace Nichols, Amryl Johnson, Zora Neale Hurston – but their publication in 1985 of *The Heart of the Race* (ed. B. Bryan, S. Dadzie and S. Scafe) did provide one of the few source books on Black women's lives in Britain. It is an essential book for all women concerned about racism and the position of Black women in Britain today. It can be read in conjunction with *Charting the Journey: Writings by Black and Third World Women* (Sheba: 1988), a collection of fiction, prose and poetry, by women from Asia, the Caribbean, Africa, Chile and Palestine. *Charting the Journey* expands and develops many of the debates around racism, anti-semitism, heterosexism and sexism, using the authors' personal life journeys to draw out and examine points at issue, and to move towards a potential coalition politics. It contains 'A Reappraisal of The Heart of the Race' by Sisters in Study, and the two books form a continuum of Black experience and debate.

Apart from the women's presses, the only other publishers who have concerned themselves with Black women's writing have been community presses like Centerprise, Peckham Bookplace, and individuals, often involved in adult education, who have printed short runs of usually autobiographical writing.

The effect of these publishing ventures, though excellent and encouraging in themselves, has not removed the writing of Black women in Britain from the margins of overall culture. As a result, it is difficult to discern clear themes and styles developing, though there are perceptible differences from writing from America. One example of this is the different engagement characters have with White society and the sense of isolation and loneliness this often brings about. Joan Riley's novels exemplify this well: Hyacinth, in *The Unbelonging*, is friendless and powerless both against White society and at home, where her father beats her and sexually assaults her. Her only escape is into dreams of a Jamaica she remembers as a place of sunshine and happiness – the reality when she returns is harsh and disturbing.

This engagement and the conflict it produces is there too in the writing of Black women involved in the women's movement and struggling for recognition of their own feminism against the racist assumptions of an all-encompassing sisterhood of White women. Again poetry provides strong examples in Carmen Williams' 'White Woman Hey' (*Feminist Review* 17, 1984: 79) and Jackie Kay's poem, 'We Are Not All Sisters under the Same Moon' (*A Dangerous Knowing* 1984), and it can also be discerned in Barbara Burford's *The Threshing Floor* (1984 – also published by Sheba), particularly in the title story.

The influences of Caribbean culture can be found in the writing of women who were born in the Caribbean, but now live and work in Britain. It is also there for women who visit the Caribbean for the first time, after years of listening to family and friends talking. And talking, and the oral traditions of storytelling, are important factors in this writing. Language features significantly in writing about the Caribbean, both in the use of Creole and patois, and in the attitudes towards non-standard English prevalent in British society and education. Writers like Jean Breeze and Merle Collins combine their knowledge of Creole in the Caribbean with its British Black version, looking back to writers like Louise Bennett. Merle Collins particularly uses her awareness of a Caribbean past reaching back to Africa ('Movements' in *Because the Dawn Breaks* 1985: 58–62); of the effects of racist education on her people ('The Lesson' in Collins 1985: 15–22); of liberation struggles in her native Grenada and throughout the world ('Callaloo' in Collins 1985: 23–6); and of the subtle racisms of Britain ('No Dialects Please' in *Watchers and Seekers* Cobham et al. 1987: 118–19). She is also concerned with the struggle of women against male domination ('How Times Have Changed' in Cobham et al. 1987: 59–60), and above all, and most centrally, with the power of language. Her poetry, and her novel *Angel* (1987) bear the strong rhythms and power of Grenadian patois, intertwining themes of liberation, history and women's struggle and continuing and embodying the oral traditions of the past into contemporary cultural forms.

Questions of language also arise for women writers for whom English is not the first language. Translation of one language into another with very different cultural forms may create erroneous impressions. In their introduction, the editors of *Right of Way* make the following comments:

> Some of us found it difficult to appreciate the translations of Urdu or Bengal poetry. Anglicised responses to the style being flowery or sentimental demanded discussion and contextualisation. Short stories which were rooted in the literary traditions of the subcontinent were considered to have abrupt endings; further discussion revealed that the marked ambiguity of our endings was common to our literary traditions.
>
> (Asian Women Writers Workshop 1988: 3)

Occasionally bilingual versions are given, as in Centerprise's anthology of Asian women's writing, *Breaking the Silence,* or the collection of Irish writing, *Wildish Things,* but this can be an expensive process. The problem, too, is that for some words and concepts, there is no translation: the idea or experience has such a different meaning and value in the respective language.

Language is a highly significant marker of identity and power, and the use a writer makes of language is charged with meaning about her own self-definition. The Jamaican writer Louise Bennett waxes lyrical and is very compelling in her performances on the subject: English was *derived from* Latin and French and Old English, but Jamaican is a *corruption* of English. With great humour she describes attitudes to Jamaican English and standard English in poems like 'Dry Foot Bwoy' and 'Non Lickle Accent'. It is writers like Louise Bennett, Merle Collins and Jean Breeze, who are also performers, who enable us, through their recordings and performances, to become accustomed to the rhythms and idioms of their English, and thus learn to appreciate it.

There can be no excuse for not tackling non-standard forms of English, any more than there is for not 'tackling' Black literature. To quote from Audre Lorde:

> All too often, the excuse given is that the literatures of women of color can only be taught by colored women, or that they are too difficult to understand, or that classes cannot 'get into' them because they come out of experiences that are 'too different'. I have heard this argument presented by white women

of otherwise quite clear intelligence, women who seem to have no trouble at all teaching and reviewing work that comes out of the vastly different experiences of Shakespeare, Molière, Dostoyevsky, and Aristophanes. Surely there must be some other explanation.

(Lorde 1984: 117)

It is important that as tutors we take the initiative in presenting, celebrating and exploring the writing of women from different cultures and experiences. This means identifying, recognising and acknowledging differences and surrendering privilege to enable Black and white women, heterosexual and lesbian women, Irish and Jewish women to begin to work together. It is a project moving beyond reactive anti-racism to positive stances where 'equal but different' can have real meaning, rather than the liberal and false assumption it currently often is. It is a project envisioned in books like *Charting the Journey*, and in Bulkin, Pratt and Smith: *Yours in Struggle* (Long Haul Press [no delusions here] 1984) and in Conlon, da Silva and Wilson: *The Things that Divide Us*.

The former is a collection of three essays by respectively, a white, Jewish lesbian, a white southern feminist, and a Black feminist. All are writers actively involved in pushing the boundaries of lesbian and feminist awareness; all are committed to dialogue across lines of class, race and colour. The essays examine the politics of identity, engaging with the complexities of interconnecting strands of oppression (e.g. the differing causes and connotations of Black and white anti-semitism; and Jewish racism). By putting such writing together in one book, by their dialogues with each other, the three writers are developing new and more challenging connections between women, acknowledging and working on difference, while going beyond it to a unity of purpose.

The Things That Divide Us performs a similar role in fiction. The three white editors, with enormous support and help from a mixed race/class/colour advisory board, collected the stories from all over America. The following extracts from the Introduction indicate the aims:

Diversity, difference, division, divisiveness. The things that divide us.

This is an anthology of fiction by women that addresses both the positive aspects of diversity among women and the

79

destructive effects of misunderstanding and separation . . .
The things that divide us can define us and help us claim
ourselves; they can also be used against us, as ways of keeping
us separate from each other and powerless. Only by writing
and talking our differences can we begin to bridge them.

(Conlon, da Silva, Wilson 1986: 7–12)

ISSUES OF SEXUALITY

Heterosexism awareness

Heterosexism, probably the least understood and most pervasive
of oppressions, comes a long way down the ladder of priorities
for action. All the '-isms', as we have indicated, tend to polarise
oppressor and oppressed, and make minorities into victims without
always examining how oppressors are also diminished by their
roles. Heterosexism, however, affects everybody, although clearly
some groups are more obviously discriminated against than others.

Heterosexism sees heterosexuality as the only right and proper
way to be. Economically, socially and politically, heterosexual
behaviour is inextricably linked, in western capitalist society, with
the nuclear family: which ideally includes marriage, a small number
of children living with their parents in an owner-occupied house,
with as many consumer durables as possible, the father in full-time
work, and the mother working part-time once the children go to
school. Marital fidelity, at least on the part of the wife, is assumed,
but it is now accepted that some marriages will fail, with divorce
now easier and cheaper to obtain than previously. Re-marriage is
no longer frowned upon; the Church of England is reviewing its
prohibition on the remarriage of divorced partners. Children are
believed to need both a mother and a father to enable them to grow
up healthily and replicate their heterosexual models.

The reality is, of course, somewhat different. Many men are
now long-term unemployed, many households rely on a wife's
full-time salary. One in four births take place outside wedlock.
The divorce rate rises every year. High house prices and a vir-
tual standstill in public sector house building has increased the
number of homeless people – to 75,000 in 1990 within London.
Changes within the Department of Social Security make it harder
for young people to leave home. These are the effects of living

under a family-orientated, enterprise-encouraging government. A few more thoughts: child sexual abuse, child assault and murder, rape, sexual assault of women, violence against women inside and outside the home, are major problems of our time. In most cases they take place within a heterosexual context.

Heterosexism is not just about prejudice against lesbians and gay men. It underpins all social relationships within our society: sexism and attitudes towards women, whether they are straight or lesbian; attitudes towards children. It affects singleee parents, single people in general, people living communally or in extended families, children in care and their parents, independent women, non-biological parents – just as much as it affects lesbians and gays. It can also affect women trapped in violent situations with men, women seeking to abort unwanted children, victims of rape and sexual assault, elderly women, mentally handicapped women.

Heightening general awareness of heterosexism is difficult, challenging and painful work. Heterosexism is such a deeply internalised, often subconscious system of belief, that most people – whatever their sexuality – find it a difficult concept to come to terms with. Becoming aware often undercuts one's sense of security; many lesbians have experienced the feeling of 'making things up as you go along' when developing relationships, and heterosexism does provide rules of a sort for everybody, which challenging questions and invalidates. Adrienne Rich's 'Compulsory Heterosexuality and Lesbian Existence', published in *Blood, Bread and Poetry* (Virago: 1987) remains one of the most significant pieces of writing in this area. It examines the pull of compulsory heterosexuality for women who are trying to explore their feminism with other women; it encapsulates many of the omissions and denials we all make in our assumptions and prejudices; and it illustrates, through the idea of a continuum, how sexuality can vary and develop throughout our lives.

At the end of this section we shall include some suggestions for beginning work on heterosexism awareness, and stereotyping in general.

Teaching lesbian issues

Teaching issues of lesbian sexuality and lesbian writing poses difficulties unlike those encountered when dealing with racism

81

in one fundamental aspect: it is perfectly possible to ignore the subject altogether because of its invisibility.

This invisibility cloaks students, tutors, and writing. It is virtually impossible, and politically quite unacceptable, for a Black or coloured woman to be anything other than she is, and indeed has been since birth. Heterosexism also operates from conception, setting up conditioned attitudes, expectations, behaviours and responses but a woman's position within the heterosexist society will change through life, depending on age, race, status, education, class, and physical ability, and to a certain extent she may be able to exercise some choice in her relation to that society.

There is, inevitably, debate (usually outside the lesbian community) as to whether lesbians are born or made; the government's inclusion of Section 28, which legislates against the promotion of homosexuality, in its Local Government Act in 1989 clearly indicates a preference for the latter point of view, but whatever the causes may be – and to lesbians they often seem ludicrously irrelevant – the realisation that she is a lesbian may occur at any time in a woman's life. Moreover, the realisation of her sexual identity will usually be internal and private, unlike one's recognition of one's gender, colour, or class, which is reflected back and confirmed by society at large. Lesbian identity can remain unrecognised by the rest of the world for years, or even a lifetime. In this respect – and this is a situation that almost all lesbians will painfully recognise – lesbian identity can be a wholly negative experience. In her paper 'Dyke in Academe 11', collected as part of *Lesbian Studies*, edited by Margaret Cruikshank, Paula Bennett sums up:

> It is the experience of the closet, of a void created by fear on one side and silence on the other. It produces a form of oppression that comes not from the things people do, *but what they do not do*. At best, this experience leads to feelings of anger, and alienation. At worst, it produces an attitude of apathy and indifference.
>
> (Cruikshank 1982: 4)

Lesbianism was not an immediate issue in the early days of the women's movement in this country. It was not mentioned in the original demands of the movement (which mainly centred on the right to choose *vis-à-vis* bearing children and childcare and demands for social equality). Discussions around sexuality in, for example, *Spare Rib*, focused on heterosexuality, on orgasms and improving relationships with men, and the occasional articles about and/or by lesbians tended to provoke angry letters about the magazine being taken over by lesbians. This attitude still prevails.

Highly acclaimed literary criticism, such as Elaine Showalter's *A Literature of their Own*, and Ellen Moers' *Literary Women*, both published in 1978, omitted lesbians, as well as Black and working-class women. Throughout much of the 1970s lesbians within the women's movement seemed as invisible as they were within society as a whole.

Although there were many lesbians involved in the women's movement (and many more who weren't), they were there as women rather than lesbians. In fact, lesbianism tended to be viewed as at best a red herring, and at worst as a serious threat which affected not only individual straight women, but also called into question the credibility of the women's movement as a whole. The standard reaction of men faced by assertive women is to accuse them of being lesbians, and this is apparently considered such an insult that few women were prepared to lay themselves open to such an accusation.

It was not easy being a lesbian in the early 1970s. Only a few years had passed since the (limited) decriminalisation of sexual acts between men (1967) and the scandals around Guy Burgess and Tony Vassall were still very much in common memory. Lesbians were still under Queen Victoria's interdict at the time of sexual law reform in the late nineteenth century, and novels published in the late 1960s (e.g. Maureen Duffy: *The Microcosm*, Panther 1967, and Pat Arrowsmith, *Somewhere Like This*, Panther 1970) reflect the underground 'twilight' nature of lesbian life. Elizabeth Smart's review, quoted on the back of the Panther edition of *The Microcosm*, sums it up:

> The tragic, trivial, consuming, passionate world of the les-
> bians, tortured by love and jealousy, harassed by poetry, and
> absolutely riddled with pain . . .

The alternatives for lesbians who wished to be actively involved in campaigning were either organisations like the Campaign for Homosexual Equality (CHE – mainly concerned with law reform and therefore mostly male) and the Gay Liberation Front (GLF – more radical, influenced by American movements, still predomi-nantly male), or the women's movement – but in the latter lesbians were invisible or isolated. Early writings such as *The Body Politic* (ed. M. Wandor: Stage 1 1972) have little to say about lesbians and that little is often far from positive:

> It is my opinion that there is a movement towards homosexuality amongst women which will continue to grow *until men completely accept women's sexual responses and the inequalities of the marriage scene disappear*
> (Whiting in Wandor (ed.) 1972: 211, our emphasis)

It was not until 1974 that the women's movement acknowledged lesbians by including the Sixth Demand, which spoke out against discrimination against lesbians, and for a self-defined sexuality for all women. (It was to be some years before theories of heterosexism began to appear.)

In the late 1970s and early 1980s women's liberation changed radically. Men, previously viewed as flawed but reformable, came increasingly to be seen as the enemy, as more and more women bore witness to the violence and hatred of men against women. Reclaim the Night marches, Women's Aid and Women Against Violence Against Women – WAVAW – campaigns moved to the centre of the women's movement, and the nature of a sexuality that seemed to produce rape, battering, murder and child sexual abuse became itself a matter of concern and study. Many women felt that any co-operation with men, whether sexual or otherwise, was a betrayal of all women, and lesbianism seemed like a viable, if not the only, alternative. In 1979 the Leeds Revolutionary Feminist Group produced their papers on political lesbianism. These were circulated in an internal newsletter and later collected as *Love Your Enemy?* which was published in 1981. These papers provoked enormous discussion and immense hostility and splits within women's movement networks. Lesbianism had finally 'come out' in the British women's movement. Throughout the early 1980s *Spare Rib*'s workers and readers were split by accusations of anti-lesbianism and misrepresentation (soon to be followed by accusations of racism and anti-semitism), and this split reflected much of the fear and anger felt by heterosexual women and amongst lesbians at this time.

These divisions within the women's movement were not simply between heterosexual women and lesbians. The lesbian community itself, never homogeneous, was, and remains, riven by conflicts between 'political' and 'non-political' lesbians, between separatists and 'collaborators', between pro- and anti-censorship lesbians, between S-M dykes and proponents of 'vanilla' sex. As these differences hardened, they were characterised as splits between revolutionary feminism and socialist feminism, both now terms that, within the lesbian community, it is hard to define.

Lesbians have often been in the forefront of active feminist campaigning; as feminism becomes more beleaguered under the pressures of survival, it is hardly surprising that those who feel themselves on the front line begin to break away and retreat into a form of sectarianism. As tutors it may not be necessary to engage with the various complex debates in full detail, but we should be able to present those debates – which have repercussions for all women.

It is important to remember at this point that lesbianism is often not the only issue affecting women's lives, and this significant fact has implications for our teaching. Equally, lesbianism is no more of a homogeneous existence than is being a woman.

Lesbianism itself, and particularly issues around sexuality and sexual practice, became the focal points of discussion in the mid-1980s. In 1983 a conference on sexuality and sexual practice was held in London in an attempt to begin airing some of the questions that had arisen around pornography and sado-masochism in America. Many women who attended the conference found it deeply intimidating; others found it tame and unfocused. The issues have remained central and often very divisive amongst lesbians: recent publications such as Joan Nestle's *A Restricted Country* 1988, *Serious Pleasure* 1989 and Sheila Jeffreys' *anticlimax* 1990 have provoked further divisions and hostility. Attitudes, particularly in London, have become sharply polarised, and attempts to discuss sexuality and sexual practice have often resulted in continued silence through fear of not following the correct line or being radical enough. Outside the large and volatile lesbian communities of London and other large cities, these issues have sometimes seemed self-indulgent and trivial when compared with everyday struggles for existence and self-determination.

Another issue has seriously affected lesbians over the last few years: the spread of AIDS, and the linking of the disease and of HIV-related illness with gay men. For some time, lesbians were viewed as being in a 'low-risk' category, and in general were either not considered at all or were tacitly included when people talked about the 'Gay Plague'. But the spread of HIV, the government's delayed and inadequate response, and the anger of gay men have all served to put lesbians in an ambivalent situation. Women have long suffered from sex-related diseases (venereal disease, cervical cancer) and questions of safer sex are of concern to all women. Many lesbians with children are naturally concerned about their children's sexual futures, and lesbians whose children were conceived by donor, often as a result of arrangements with gay male friends, are concerned about whether they and their children are at risk from AIDS. In this particularly, some lesbians feel more naturally allied to gay men than to heterosexual women.

Some of the same issues arose when the government introduced Section 28 of the Local Government Act 1989. Again the question of allying ourselves with gay men, if only by going on the same marches, became urgent. Some lesbians took their own actions (abseilling in Parliament, disrupting BBC News broadcasts) but many also refused to participate in protests including gay men. Another dismaying factor was how often heterosexual women failed to recognise the emotions of lesbians in response to the government's threat against us, or to acknowledge that such legislation created an atmosphere in which attacks against lesbians and gay men of whatever nature seemed to receive official sanction.

This brief overview should indicate that lesbians are not and have never been automatically included within the women's movement and Women's Studies courses. Exclusion has not only limited awareness of the variety of women's experience, but has meant that significant aspects of feminist theory have also been omitted. It is primarily lesbians who have pioneered the study of the nature of heterosexism and patriarchy. Significant writers such as Adrienne Rich, Audre Lorde, Mary Daly and Judy Grahn are essential to any understanding of current feminist thinking. Writers as diverse as Sheila Jeffreys, Andrea Dworkin, Joan Nestle and Pat Califia are central to current debates on pornography and censorship, role-playing and sado-masochism.

The question, as with all areas of difference, becomes: how best to ensure that lesbian experience and lesbian voices are represented within Women's Studies courses? And here the problem of invisibility needs to be faced. For it is still too often the assumption that people are heterosexual unless they state otherwise; and coming out is not always easy or even possible. Heterosexual women may react adversely to lesbians; lesbians themselves may not feel able, whether because of external pressures or internal fear, to speak their sexuality. A prerequisite of any Women's Studies group should therefore be a clear statement of inclusion and respect for all women whatever their sexuality. Moreover, this needs to be quite specific and not merely sweeping; the history and position of lesbians within the women's movement means that there are few aspects of women's experience on which there is not a lesbian perspective. The pornography/censorship debate has already been mentioned; recent work in lesbian history is now being published: *Not a Passing Phase* by the Lesbian History Group, *Inventing Ourselves* by the Hall-Carpenter Archives, to complement the earlier work of Sheila Jeffreys and Lillian Faderman. No course on mothers and daughters would be complete without examining Adrienne Rich's *Of Woman Born* and considering the position of lesbian mothers; many of the significant poets currently writing are lesbians – including Judy Grahn, Adrienne Rich, Audre Lorde, Irena Klepfisz, U. A. Fanthorpe. In Britain two important collections of lesbian poetry and polemic appeared in 1988: *Naming the Waves* ed. C. McEwen and *Out the Other Side* ed. S. O'Sullivan and C. McEwen, both published by Virago. They bring together significant contemporary writing from both sides of the Atlantic, and indicate the depth and breadth of Lesbian Studies at the present time.

Our own experience of teaching Women's Studies classes reflects the advantages and disadvantages of the integrationist approach. Throughout our courses we included writing by lesbians in every course we taught. Our main aim was simply that of inclusion as part of the process of breaking down the barriers of isolation and invisibility. But within our groups it proved to be very difficult to discuss lesbian contributions to any given subject as specifically lesbian rather than as simply another woman's contribution. At times, we had to point out what we felt were anti-lesbian aspects of some writing, as, for example, the treatment of Mike in Alison Fell's *Every Move You Make*; the treatment of lesbians throughout the writing of Maya Angelou. In a group of lesbians and non-lesbians, where the tutors themselves are lesbians, it can become very easy to guilt trip the non-lesbians by pointing out such things; this has never been our intention, but such feelings quickly indicate the gaps in experience and awareness within a group. At the same time, other lesbians may feel threatened by a mixed group, and this too has been our experience.

Sometimes it worked well, as when we were discussing Judy Grahn's poem 'A Woman is Talking to Death'. This was towards the end of the course entitled 'Women and Poetry: Questions of Identity', in the session on writing as a lesbian. (The course itself is discussed in more detail in the poetry chapter.) The discussion of Grahn's poem, coming as it did after some weeks of close textual and contextual study, focused on two questions:

1 Could the poem have been written by a non-lesbian woman, and how did it affect us that it was written by a lesbian?
2 What did we understand by 'lesbian' and 'lesbian poetry'?

The poem is about women loving and caring for each other, and the ways in which external pressures work to make women betray each other. Its immediate context is a motorcycle accident witnessed by two lesbians, in which a reckless motorcyclist is killed and a Black man is questioned by the police. The unreliability of the women's witness is starkly made, and the poem explores the idea of women bearing witness in a much wider sense. It is intensely powerful and moving, and in the United States it has become a sort of anthem amongst lesbians – mentioned in fictional writing, for instance, as a turning-point and a great strength in women's lives. We read it aloud, as it should be read, and the woman who was most affected by it was not a lesbian. She felt that she couldn't appreciate it fully because it described experiences that she could imagine sympathetically, but could never know. At the same time, she was emphatic in her belief that it was written for, and should be read by, all women, and that it was saying something very important for all women.

On the other hand, one of the lesbians in the group was unclear why this particular poem was seen as being lesbian. Her response reflects a common uncertainty about coupling the word 'lesbian' with 'writing'. This was an issue we had occasionally tried to raise, being concerned that terms like 'lesbian writing' could isolate and ghettoise writing by lesbians. It also begged the questions: is all writing by lesbians *per se* lesbian writing? Do only lesbian themes make lesbian writing? Who defines 'lesbian' anyway?

Partly in an attempt to resolve some of these difficulties, we have, over the last few years, begun to work less within Women's Studies and more in Lesbian Studies. A move which raises yet more questions, for example, surely Lesbian Studies is part of Women's Studies? This was a difficult decision; as teachers we feel that education is a powerful force for change, and that change will only come about if everyone is exposed to different ideas and attitudes.

Women's Studies, even now, has little credibility in the academic world, and what it has, has only been gained by women struggling to make their voices heard within a male-dominated system. That struggle could scarcely have taken place without women grabbing space and support from and for themselves. How much more, then, do more marginalised groups like lesbians need that space and support to define their history, politics and culture?

Our move was also influenced by wanting to work in an area where we did not have to be constantly coming out and explaining oppression. Once a woman who had known both of us in various contexts for some months, and knew we were both lesbians, declared to the group that she didn't know any lesbians. On another occasion, a student hurled a book of lesbian short stories across the room, announcing loudly her hope that there were none of those perverts in the class. The fact of their lesbianism is one of the hardest things for lesbians to say and one of the easiest things for non-lesbians to forget. Moreover, there were debates within the lesbian community, particularly around pornography and censorship, gender roles and sado-masochism that we felt we needed to be part of, and that couldn't be integrated into more general courses. We feel now that working separately has considerably strengthened and reinforced our ability to live and work as lesbians within a heterosexist society.

IMAGES AND STEREOTYPING

Exercises

One of the easiest ways to begin working on Differences is through exercises involving images and stereotyping. Here are two examples that have proved useful in the past.

Families

Collect a group of photographs, black and white, or in colour, of individuals, couples (same and opposite sex), groups, including children with people of differing ages e.g. a child with a man, a group of children with two women; children with an older person, children with a man and a woman, etc. All ages and ethnic groups should be represented. (The pack on families produced by ALBSU has an A3 sheet of such photographs.)

Either: present all the images to the group and ask them to say which are in families, and why they think this.

Or: ask members to choose pictures and say whether they would describe them as a family or not, and why.

This exercise is useful for beginning to think about heterosexism, and our own assumptions about what is a family. Material gathered can be used to create definitions and consider how much they come from our own experience, are culturally specific, have changed over time, and so on.

Stereotyping

Collect photographs from newspapers and magazines of events and situations. They should involve a number of people – parties, meetings, funerals, incidents of various types can be used. The pictures need to contain clearly defined individuals and be large enough to cut into smaller pieces. Use a jigsaw technique to isolate individual, background, signs and so on. The pieces may need to be stuck on card to be used over again.

Then in groups give out one piece of the jigsaw and ask people what it represents. It may be a wide-eyed Asian child, thin, dressed in white; or a group of Black people dancing and singing; a white skinhead in an aggressive, mobile attitude.

As the group comments on each piece, someone should take notes. Gradually the picture is built up and members become aware of the ways in which their image memory has led them to stereotype. e.g. the Asian child was at a birthday party, not a famine or disaster victim; the Black people were at a funeral in South Africa; the skinhead was about to rescue someone from falling masonry.

The exercise can be used to introduce any work on stereotyping and difference awareness.

Variations on both of these can include using pictures of women and asking questions like:

Does she have children?
Does she work in an office?

DIFFERENCES

Does she work in a factory?
Is she married?
Does she have a university degree?
Does she drive a car?
Does she live alone? etc.

4

SENSES OF THE PAST

TEACHING LITERATURE AND HISTORY

In this section, we set out the issues we had to consider when we decided to include non-contemporary writing in our courses. The issues were of two distinct kinds. First, our courses were often attended by students who hadn't had much in the way of education after the age of sixteen. This meant we couldn't assume they shared the same referential knowledge of literature that we did. We also couldn't assume their interest in the past. Second, our understanding of culture and writing had been transformed through the radical critiques of feminism, anti-racism and socialism. We were conscious that the heritage of English Literature, with its many exclusions, was not necessarily of great use or value to our students. The processes and arguments we engaged in, between ourselves and through the classes we taught, affirmed our belief in the importance of extending the work we did to include a historical dimension. That historical dimension, however, had to include difference: to be histories rather than history.

Our culture maintains a very distinctive sense of history, in which the past is conditional upon the present, and constantly rewritten to serve changing needs. In contemporary conservatism, the past is being re-invented as the morality of the future: the return to Victorian Values, Black or Third World, Irish, Jewish or working-class history is told, where it is told at all, from viewpoints and interests which are not our own, and tend to confirm our powerlessness and lack of worth. If we are lesbians, the problem is compounded further: our past appears not to exist at all.

We found the historical approach to women's writing wasn't popular. Students sometimes consider it harder than reading and discussing contemporary writers. It is true that it frequently involves reading work which contains irrelevant or unpalatable ideas and assumptions; its selection and presentation falls more to the tutor and cuts across attempts at self-determined learning or other forms of democratising student involvement. Is it best left alone, deemed to be outside the interests of any but those engaged upon the study of literature for a qualification: work, rather than pleasure, be it a GCSE or a degree? Should our teaching be organised around whatever, and however, random a collection of books women, and tutors, have found interesting, enjoyable and illustrative of conflict and experiences within their own lives? Should we stress personal identification and empathy over and above any attempt to relate books to each other and to the processes of writing and publishing? Or should that moment of personal recognition be extended to develop the historical dimensions of the theme under consideration?

We believe that a substantial component of any oppression is the denial of history, which itself helps to maintain subordination and distortions of that history. It is necessary, therefore, to find ways of taking history on board. The ideas which follow are drawn from our experiences of teaching. We began by using a significant proportion of historical material (see section on courses); gradually moved away from using historical material at all and finally returned it to the course in a quite different form.

One powerful factor keeping us with contemporary authors was wanting to expand the range of experience represented. Current politics centred on expanding the term 'Woman'; demonstrating how it contained a variety of expectations and experiences depending on class, age, race or sexuality. We didn't want to be trapped into taking a few stock lives as normative. This was a theme and motivation in contemporary writing and publishing too, so it seemed important to consider it. Had we wanted to trawl back for that representativeness we would have met problems.

Even if women in the past had been able to express their sense of being Black, lesbian or working class in a written form, publication posed a significant barrier. At the same time, because our education had been in the dominant opinions and prejudices of our culture, we would not necessarily know where to look for oppositional writing in the past. As these traditions are unearthed, we can begin to construct the specific history of Black, women's, working-class or lesbian writing. Once this work is in progress it is possible to utilise it in various ways, but sadly the degree of primary research entailed often puts this work outside the scope of Adult Education groups and tutors. Even then we may find that the books have gone out of print. The limited access to copyright libraries and the restrictions on and expenses of photocopying, all work towards limiting the availability of this material.

The issue is not just what is not present in the writing of the past, or the absence of writing itself, it is also the more challenging question of what is there. How do we respond to expressions of homophobia, racism and class prejudice in books which are important and powerful components of the women's literary tradition? Racism and class prejudice in *The Well of Loneliness*, class prejudice in Virginia Woolf's writing, anti-semitism in much of the 'golden age' of women's detective writing in the 1920s and 1930s? Clearly, to respond as we initially did – avoiding the problem entirely by not using the books at all – is not a solution.

Another consideration in keeping our choice of books for study in the present related less to the material than to how we studied it. Because books from the past exist within a critical discourse, our approach to them also involves engaging with those opinions and judgements. It is hard to trust our response and evaluation of work by, for example, Virginia Woolf or Charlotte Brontë because of the weight of critical opinion they carry. Even if we disagree with that opinion, it still functions as a guide to us. No such body of opinion has been formulated or fixed around contemporary writing. Learning to trust your own judgement about books, gaining the confidence to analyse, compare and interpret freely, was valuable work to be doing with our students.

LANGUAGE AND STYLE

During the last fifteen years feminism has developed a style which is non-literary, direct and immediate. This made it accessible to a wide readership. We do not have to go very far back before we encounter works which are obviously not contemporary, written in a style which seems cumbersome, wordy, pretentious. One of the first tasks in approaching historical writers can, literally, be helping people to read. There is a greater than usual need to slow down, to read passages once or twice and preferably aloud in order to get the rhythm or nuances correct. It is useful to discuss the style and anticipate what, by being strange or unusual, may cause problems.

For instance, many people find nineteenth- and early twentieth-century novels over-full of descriptive passages, preferring more recent work where description is done more suggestively. While a discussion about why this should be the case will not necessarily make it any easier to read, it may encourage the effort. Our familiarity with images, especially through film and television makes it difficult to understand a world which lacked such visual complexity. Imagining a world where we do not have a repertoire of images with which to flesh out sparse written descriptions can make it easier to understand how writers were responding to the reader's need to see a world.

But style need not be just a problem, it can be actively incorporated into the learning process. Language which appears fixed and of the moment is itself the repository of change, the site of struggle over meaning and value. To focus in on language, to chart its changes, is a powerful way of involving students in the continuity of the past. The sanctioning of what can and cannot be said about women's lives is partly a question of what language exists, and what it will and will not stand. Using examples, such as Emily Brontë's *Wuthering Heights* or Elizabeth Barrett Browning's *Aurora Leigh*, where there was shock or outrage at the time that women could write on such subjects in such a fashion, can be valuable. Presenting the work to students in this light – as something that was challenging and original at the time – can ease its comprehension in the present.

Similarly, it can be helpful to discuss what it means to speak of certain subjects, especially those taboo areas of female, bodily experience, and how that expression changes between friends, children and parents. That perception of change can be used as the basis for extending the discussion back in time, acknowledging the differences of class, race and dialect in language and for thinking about what can be said privately and publicly.

It is always worth spending some time talking about language as language. This will be greatly eased if you have access to materials dealing with the historical development of English, especially the contestations which contain and demarcate its various standard and non-standard varieties. An impressive collection of teaching materials developed through ILEA's Language and Literacy Unit, *Language and Power* (Harcourt Brace Jovanovich 1990) make this much easier. Considerable feminist thinking, too, has gone into the ways in which language reflects, constructs and re-presents women's position and this can provide challenging sessions in their own right, as well as opening up writing from the past for discussion.

For all the difficulties we have outlined, we continue to maintain the importance of developing a historical approach. A lot of the problems associated with the past are re-formulated if we stop thinking of it as The Past and ask Which Past?

Disenchantment with narrow versions of the past associated with history learnt in school or the laborious chronologies of academic English is all too understandable. If we approach history less as a series of facts, dates and discrete, significant events and more as a process involving change and conflict, standing in relation to our lives, there is scope for a more dynamic engagement. Similarly, if we change the subjects of history we learn about a new experience of the world, but must also ask why and how it has been excluded. 'Which past?' and 'Whose history?', asked from the perspective just of women, or of working-class, Black or lesbian women; opens up whole new areas of connection and comparison. The challenge, as teachers, is to find ways of approaching the past, understanding it and communicating its relevance.

TRADITIONS

Tradition is both the gathering in, and existence of, a set of beliefs, customs and practices and the active perpetuation, the handing on of them. In literary terms, it includes certain authors, their works and a set of values and assumptions about them. Some of the assumptions and values are clearly stated, others implicit. It is a highly constructed process that presents itself as natural and consensual. It is also exclusively concerned with criticism, the production of literature is not at issue. That too, is seen as a natural, inevitable process in which real writers will always emerge, whatever the odds. Needless to say, the tradition turns out to be white, middle-class and though male-dominated, reserves a place for women.

That there are women within the canons of great, national writing is both pleasurable sustenance and occasion for despair. The existence of some women writers tempers the exclusion of most women, strengthening the idea that if only you, or they, were good enough. . . . They are used, as Tillie Olsen writes,

> to rebuke ('to be models'); to imply the unrealistic, see it can be done, all you need is capacity and will.
>
> (Olsen 1980: 39)

What the presence of women, so few women, among them Jane Austen, George Eliot, Charlotte and Emily Brontë and Virginia Woolf, in the literary tradition has done is signal possibility, to make visible women's ambition and accomplishment. But this has been, besides a very partial rendering of the extent and circumstances of that achievement, at the expense of a full, contextualised account of how women relate to the literary tradition, how the constitution of the literary tradition determines the possibilities for writing women. Conventional literary canonisations are orientated towards the consumption of literature: what to read, how to read it and what to think about it. The criticism which follows from such a position is not connected to any practice of contemporary writing.

The history of women as writers has been one of the most significant projects to have emerged in the last fifteen years. Elaine Showalter's impressive account of British novelists from 1800 to the 1970s can be criticised on a number of theoretical, methodological and cultural counts; what is exemplary about the text is its documentation of writing as a profession for women. Elaine Showalter does not de-centre the women of the great tradition, but rather fills in 'the minor novelists, who were the links in the chain' (Showalter 1977: 7). Our understanding of the project as feminist criticism would entail a completely new drawing of the map.

The questions which underpin her research establish and help us understand that there is a distinct history of women engaged in the profession of letters:

> I have needed to ask why women began to write for money and how they negotiated the activity of writing within their families. What was their professional self-image? How was their work received, and what effects did criticism have upon them? What were their experiences as women, and how were these reflected in their books? What was their understanding of womanhood? What were their relationships to other women, to men and to their readers? How did changes in women's status affect their lives and careers? And how did the vocation of writing itself change the women who committed themselves to it?
>
> (Showalter 1977: 12–13)

As the basis for empirical research, these indicators are sound and they have influenced subsequent feminist criticism. *Writing for Their*

Lives by Gillian Hanscombe and Virginia Smyers, for example, is a brilliant account of modernist women writers which is organised partly as a case study using these sorts of questions to structure the presentation of their extensive material.

The question of tradition, though, is more complex than can be dealt with by staying within the parameters of The Great Tradition, albeit a more comprehensive account of its composition regarding women. If we return to that sense of tradition as necessary knowledge gathered and handed on, it becomes clear that we need to know a lot more about women's writing than the way it acquires classic literary status.

Throughout the nineteenth and early twentieth centuries, many women saw in writing a powerful way to plead causes rooted in social and political struggle. In some cases fiction was the most effective way to put across ideas and experiences, as in Harriet Beecher Stowe's *Uncle Tom's Cabin*, which did much to build a popular reaction against slavery in America amongst liberal whites. Other women's diaries and memoirs provided accounts of their motivation towards social change and the hardships they met with. Florence Nightingale and Mary Seacole, for example, both provided important polemic and documentary accounts of nursing's early establishment as a profession. They also record the determination of women struggling successfully against the limited expectations of them which class and race prescribed. At the same time they provide a good illustration of the partiality of history. Black people growing up in colonial Jamaica heard about Florence Nightingale, but not about Mary Seacole, their own national heroine.

Annie Besant, Marie Stopes and Margaret Sanger spent much of their lives organising, educating and promoting a better social and sexual life for women through birth control and sex education. They used the pamphlet form to reach a wider audience than their personal visiting and mass meetings could achieve. An insight into the class prejudices of the time is clearly gained in following the history of the prosecution of Marie Stopes: not for writing *Married Love*, a sex manual which gave contraceptive advice; but for encouraging its publication in a cheap edition, thus encouraging a working-class readership.

Women also claimed the profession of letters not as a means to an end but as an end in itself. Many of the women whose novels form the spine of The Great Tradition, were also active as critics. George Eliot wrote early in her career 'Silly Novels for

Lady Novelists'. It captures the contradictions of women writing in its clear impulse to establish a project quite different from the run of the mill, humiliatingly female concerns of the majority of writing women. The contradiction remains relevant to the present day, as does the idea that anti-feminism is most effectively pursued from the lips and pen of a woman whose own life and ambitions are not conventionally feminine.

For many years George Eliot was an ambiguous example to women. On the one hand she was a revered and financially successful writer who had flouted social expectations about her life style and got away with it. On the other hand, her perceived lack of social grace and beauty was taken as a warning to intellectually ambitious women of the pitfalls they faced.

George Eliot wrote without obvious connection either to contemporary or historical women writers. That such a network of working women writers existed is clear from the profusion of novels and literary memoirs they left; writers such as Mrs Oliphant, Eliza Lyn Linton, Mary Cholmondeley, Alice James, Elizabeth Robbins, Mrs Humphry Ward, whose work is now available through Virago, Pandora and The Women's Press after decades of unavailability; as well as the better known and more easily accessible work of Elizabeth Gaskell, Charlotte and Emily Brontë.

Although George Eliot set herself apart from those literary networks, historical evidence shows that they have often existed and been vital to women. These sustaining connections between women have rarely attracted the attention that accompanies groupings in which men predominate, even when they are as well documented as those from the early and mid-twentieth century in Britain have been. Gradually, feminist scholarship is beginning to explore and interpret these groupings of writers, journalists, thinkers and artists, but it has been slow work. Sheri Benstock's *Women of the Left Bank* and Gillian Hanscombe and Virginia Smyers' *Writing for their Lives* are complementary, fascinating accounts of women at the forefront of the modernist movement. As the twentieth century progressed, more opportunities, especially in journalism, opened up to women. Writers such as Storm Jameson, Winifred Holtby and Rebecca West were also active in a range of contemporary issues such as colonial independence, the peace movement and Trade Unions, and used journalism to advance their causes.

The history, though, is not one of unqualified progress. The life of Flora Thompson is a graphic indictment of the pressures which prevent women from writing, or from writing as much as they want or need to. Chilling as Flora Thompson's words are, they are made more poignant knowing that for every Flora struggling late into print, many more women took their ambitions to the grave.

Flora Thompson, 1876–1949 is best known as the author of *Lark Rise to Candleford*, a book which has all but disappeared under the welter of packaged nostalgia which exploits it to sell bed linen and bath salts. It is a trilogy of semi-fictionalised autobiography. Flora Thompson's achievement is to combine a perceptive account of her own transition from childhood to maturity with an unsentimental account of the ending of a whole way of life, that of the rural poor. In addition to this, she wrote a number of other accounts of country life and much journalism, romantic stories that sapped her creativity but, because they paid, earned her the right within her marriage to continue to write.

Flora Thompson was in her sixties when success arrived and she wrote of herself ten years later, shortly before her death:

> To be born in poverty is a terrible handicap to a writer. I often say to myself that it has taken one lifetime for me to prepare to make a start. If human life lasted 200 years I might hope to accomplish something.

Working-class women writers often come late to their writing, a pattern we still see today in authors such as Lena Kennedy, Betty Burton and Kathleen Dayus.

In looking at the ways in which women writers have formed connections between themselves, how they have interpreted their roles as writers and critics, looked to each other as models, we can begin to construct an account of women which extends far beyond the narrow template of conventional literary judgements.

Another sort of knowledge we need is first broached by Tillie Olsen in *Silences*, a book which acknowledges its debt to Elaine Showalter, and stands in a complementary rather than a competitive relation to it.

Tillie Olsen writes less as a critic than as a writer, returning to the heart of the critical project in ways which are inspirational and sustaining. If Elaine Showalter helps us to focus on what we have by way of tradition, Tillie Olsen keeps us sharply conscious of how we have come by it; of who and what has been lost on the way.

We must not speak of women writers in our century (as we

cannot speak of women in any area of recognised human achievement) without speaking also of the invisible, the as-innately-capable: the born to the wrong circumstances – diminished, excluded, foundered, silenced.

(Olsen 1980: 39)

Her work also shows that historical approaches to women's writing need to integrate the history of women as writers, the history of women as represented by women writers and their social history.

Intellectual work and scholarship is launched upon a work of re-discovery, re-claiming and re-evaluating the traditions, of women's writing. The empowering knowledge this gives is an alternative to the idea that women writers work and live in isolation.

The economics of publishing always wants some women writers for the many women readers: it is literature that excludes them. Women may write popular books which sell well and are valued at the time, but they frequently remain writers of fiction rather than literature, verse rather than poetry. This is a process which operates within, and has major implications for, history. All around us we will see women writers, women's books and be lulled into thinking the arguments have been made and battles fought. Later, when the books have been allowed to go out of print, failed to become required reading or incorporated into the present's version of the significant past, it will be too late. Later generations will not know what they have missed, nor be encouraged to ask 'Why no women?' because there will be some women, a few. Fiction, though it has always complained about it, has always had to admit the presence of women.

Where poetic traditions are concerned, as Alicia Suskin Ostriker's impressive account of the emergence of women's poetry in America, *Stealing the Language*, demonstrates, it is altogether a different matter:

> It has always been customary when praising women writers to say that they do not write like most other women. The commendatory couplets written by Bradstreet's brother-in-law began, 'If women I with women may compare, / Your works are solid, others weak as air'. T.S. Eliot concluded an essay on Marianne Moore with 'one final, and "magnificent" compliment' on her work: 'One never forgets that it is written by a woman; but . . . one never thinks of this particularly as anything but a positive virtue.'

(Ostriker 1987: 2)

Women have too often been ignored or subsumed into a literary tradition on terms that cut them off from themselves as women and from the needs of future women readers and writers. Feminism makes possible a different account of women writers.

Re-working histories of women as writers means taking women out of isolation and putting them into a context which involves connection and continuities between themselves, as women who write, and others who had or were attempting the same struggle. It involves knowing and beginning to understand the nature of women's lives as writers: what conditions support and enable, which diminish. Knowing how women put together the business of being writers: what they needed to know and how they came into that knowledge is vital to women continuing that same work. That is the real value of tradition: handing down the information which, as women, we need:

> The road was cut many years ago, as Virginia Woolf reminds us: 'by Fanny Burney, by Aphra Benn, by Harriet Martineau, by Jane Austen, by George Eliot, many famous women and many more unknown and forgotten . . . Thus, when I came to write . . . writing was a reputable and harmless occupation.'
> Predecessors, ancestors, a body of literature, an acceptance of the right to write: each in themselves an advantage.
>
> (Olsen 1980: 23)

The knowledge of women writers that we have is often not appropriate or accurate. Women's literary history is scarred by women about whom we know too much of the wrong things. Virginia Woolf is a case in point. Her reputation is patrician: a woman writer of such consummate artistry that she is detached from, above the common run of women. And, as befits such a singular talent, the possession of literary genius by a woman was accompanied by or resulted in madness. Whichever it is is irrelevant – what matters is the madness.

Popular conceptions of Virginia Woolf, even some feminist ones, obscure the extent to which her concern with women, their education, lives and achievements, was a concrete rather than abstract preoccupation. This can be seen in her famous works, *Room of One's Own* and *Three Guineas*. Her critical work as a reviewer, lecturer and as essayist in such works as *The Common Reader* shows her extensive interest in women. It shows time and again her desire to render the connections between women writers and to situate herself in relation to them. Likewise, her friendship with other women writers belies the image we have of her. That Virginia Woolf found the issue of how to relate to her female contemporaries problematic is undeniable. Her friendships and shared ambitions with women such as May Sarton, Katherine Mansfield, May Sinclair, Winifred Holtby, Vita Sackville-West and Rebecca West caused her moments of envy, jealousy and smug superiority. Later, usually male, critics and biographers have been quick to capitalise upon this. Quentin Bell's biography of Virginia Woolf has this to say about her relationship with Katherine Mansfield, a writer whose index entry asks us to 'see Murry, Katherine'.

> They were always to disagree and never to disagree finally. United by their devotion to literature and divided by their rivalry as writers, they found each other immensely attractive and yet profoundly irritating. Katherine . . . was interesting, vulnerable, gifted and charming. But also she dressed like a tart and behaved like a bitch. Or so it sometimes seemed to Virginia and in rather the same way she admired her stories, so sharply observed, so perceptive, at times so tragic and yet, at others, so cheap and so obvious. Katherine Mansfield, I think, returned Virginia's admiration and also her animosity.
>
> (Bell 1972: 37)

After all, it proves how impossible are friendships, relationships of trust and sustenance between women. The difficulties of co-operative rather than competitive relationships between women remain. The problem has not gone away, but how important it is to know that Virginia Woolf acknowledged those problems from the point of view of needing and wanting to overcome them: knowing what was good about them:

> 2 hours priceless talk – priceless in the sense that to no one else can I talk in the same disembodied way about writing . . . I enjoyed myself.
>
> 5th June 1920
>
> Katherine has been dead a week . . . when I began to write, it seemed to me there was no point in writing. Katherine won't read it. Katherine's my rival no longer . . . I was jealous of her writing – the only writing I have ever been jealous of. This made it harder to write to her . . . yet I

have the feeling that I shall think of her at intervals all through life.

16th January 1923
(Woolf 1978: 45–6 and 225–7)

Neither of these quotations are included or referred to in the Bell biography or in Leonard Woolf's compilation from Virginia's diaries, *A Writer's Diary*.

These popular misconceptions abound with almost all the women writers who achieve some measure of fame or success. Sometimes the misconceptions are linked to the particular person and what we know of them, as with Radclyffe Hall. At other times, it is the absence of a context which would illuminate and make more complex the reading of particular writers and their writing, as with Sylvia Plath.

Radclyffe Hall, *The Well of Loneliness* and the scandal of its ban under the obscenity laws in 1928 are indivisible. For many women, including many lesbians, this is all they do know of Radclyffe Hall's writing and the book is skewed, perceived as perhaps a first novel by a young, headstrong writer out to plead a cause; or it can be wrongly thought to have ended her writing career. Each assumption is wrong and it is important to understand properly where exactly *The Well of Loneliness* figures in Hall's career as a writer. She embarked upon it when firmly established, believing this would ensure her work was taken seriously. Perhaps more important, given the status of *The Well* as a definitive account of lesbianism, is to know that Radclyffe Hall wrote other, and probably better, books concerning the subject than this one. (See *The Unlit Lamp*.)

With a writer such as Sylvia Plath it is important to make students aware of the range of her work. In our own experience, for example, taught Sylvia Plath as part of a University Modern Poets Course in the early 1970s, we were directed only towards 'Lady Lazarus', 'Daddy' and 'The Applicant'. Plath was presented as mad and bad: disturbingly preoccupied with Nazism, death and suffering. Clearly, those strands are present in her work, but they need to be explained, put into a context and it also needs to be explicit that they are facets rather than the sum of her work. When we included Sylvia Plath on a course entitled 'Mothers and Daughters', students were surprised to discover that she was included not only because of her tortured relationship with

Aurelia, her own mother, but also because of her fine writing about maternity and her children. A view of Sylvia Plath as the wild girl, sexually precocious and neurotically obsessed with death cannot account for the woman who, in her poem 'Nick and the Candlesticks', sees her child as:

> the one
> solid the spaces lean on.
> (Plath 1981: 242)

and so says nothing at all about it. But with Sylvia Plath it is not just needing to know the range of her writing, the way it struggled with and against being a woman and being a poet, it is needing to know the times she lived and wrote in, the consequences of that for her as a woman and a poet. Because Plath is so close, so nearly a contemporary, it is tempting to let the lens of history slide, to assimilate her into a world that seems like, looks like our own. Nothing could be further from the case.

Plath died in 1963, before contemporary feminism and was formed in a literary culture that was both highly competitive and formalist. A world into which women, literally and metaphorically, had access only on condition that they abdicate femaleness. Outside the literary world, the 1950s and 1960s were proscribing a femininity of rigid and impossible idealism. Sylvia Plath was caught on that rack and her literary resolution of the conflict via a poetry which, as Alicia Suskin Ostriker explains, connects:

> Physical vulnerability and ironic self-rejection . . . [having] most thoroughly to have internalised the larger culture's principles of flesh-rejection and aspiration towards transcendence . . . a radical extension of the mode of disenchanted alienation.
> (Ostriker 1987: 99–103)

represents the originality and power of her achievement. Her inability to resolve the conflict satisfactorily at a personal level returns the question to history and away from individual blame or failure.

To understand and learn from Sylvia Plath, it is necessary to know her typicalities and atypicalities; to be able to balance the personal factors: an unfortunate marriage; a highly developed competitive streak, certainly fostered, if not created, by her North

American education; the pressures of unaccustomed poverty and emotional distress; with those pertaining more generally.

Perhaps the most illuminating exercise to do with Sylvia Plath is to take her away from the company of Anne Sexton, with whom she is often linked, in ways which emphasise madness and suicide as the connection between women and poetry, and put her against those other contemporaries: Denise Levertov, Adrienne Rich and Audre Lorde.

In this way, and through their own testimony about writing, and living, through the 1950s and 1960s into feminism, we ground Plath's writing in a history of women's writing. Adrienne Rich, writing of her own history as a woman poet makes two statements resonant for a study of Plath. Introducing her selected poems, she writes:

> I have not tried to remake the woman of twenty or thirty, in the light of the woman of forty-five, or to revise my earlier experience and craft because I would see, and articulate, differently today. . . . To be a woman at this time is to know extraordinary forms of anger, joy, impatience, love and hope. Poetry, words on paper, are necessary but not enough; . . . midway in my own life, I know that we have only begun.
>
> (Foreword to *Poems: Selected and New*,
> Rich 1974: xv–xvi)

Ten years later, she has a clearer sense of what the differences were and their consequences for her writing:

> One task for the nineteen- or twenty-year-old poet who wrote the earliest poems here was to learn that she was neither unique nor universal, but a person in history, a woman and not a man, a white and also Jewish inheritor of a particular Western consciousness from the making of which most women have been excluded. The learning of poetic craft was much easier than knowing what to do with it.
>
> (Foreword to *The Fact of a Door-Frame*,
> Rich 1984: xv)

This helps us realise again that Sylvia Plath's death at the age of thirty put an end to years of writing. She died, in terms of poetry, an infant. This fixes her image: as if we have been denied twenty years of Ariel's. Seeing the work of Adrienne Rich, Audre Lorde and Denise Levertov, each very different ways of working poetry, and reading what Adrienne Rich herself says about change, the realisation comes that what has been lost is the potential for change. A wholly other poetry.

Less speculative, less 'if only', is that powerful assertion: 'the learning of poetic craft was much easier than knowing what to do with it'. It is this which keys in to a reading of Sylvia Plath, picking up the undoubted stylistic brilliance of her writing, what Adrienne Rich describes as 'The powers, temptations, privileges, potential deceptions, and two-edged weapons of language' (Rich 1984: xv). One connection is that between the poet not knowing what to do with her poetic craft and a culture that cannot know, doesn't want to know, what women do with themselves.

One form of knowledge we have about women writers which it is good to re-examine, is that which comes from having read, as children, books by women which are in fact written for adults. It seems to us that this occurs far more with books by women authors and is a way of diminishing them, making them less adult. A random sampling of such work gives us: *National Velvet* by Enid Bagnold, *Jane Eyre* by Charlotte Brontë, *Wuthering Heights* by Emily Brontë, all of Jane Austen, Christina Rossetti's poems, *Uncle Tom's Cabin* by Harriet Beecher Stowe and *The Mill on the Floss* by George Eliot.

There is a value in getting back to those women authors, starting to understand why they are represented to us in partial and inaccurate ways. Jane Austen is perhaps the most extreme case in point. Some women who haven't read her, or have only read her at school perhaps for 'O' or 'A' level will argue that she is not worth reading. Boring, prim, narrow-minded, irrelevant, snobbish. They reel off the stock prejudices against her, unleavened by the standard diminishing terms of incorporation: her irony, her delicate, interior worlds.

Jane Austen is no feminist manqué, but there is more to her than the above suggests and there are, prior to a new reading of her, interesting discussions to be had about why we are encouraged to read her in those particular ways, why she is held to be a model, how the illusion of female modesty is fostered and why we are asked to value it. The actual conditions of her writing life are a case in point. Most people will tell you that she wrote in the drawing room, hiding her writing if anyone came in, accommodating herself to the interruptions. And she is praised for this meekness. She points in this, as people would have her fiction do, a lesson in manners and modest behaviour. But Jane Austen not only wrote in the privacy of her home, she also published. And she relished both the writing and its success. Her letters show her fully aware of its craft, its power to earn money as well as the preoccupying, rigorous activity it was to her.

Her actual writing is far more subtle and relevant for women than the glosses which dismiss it as superficial accounts of manners and morals. It is inevitably class-bound but there is also a ruthlessness in her satire, a clear and calculating eye cast over that most material of women's concerns at the time: marriage. One of the most illuminating and exciting critics of Jane Austen is Ellen Moers, who in *Literary Women*, both provides an inspired account of the economic preoccupations of Jane Austen's fiction and details her influence on future generations of women writers:

> lack of interest in Austen's concern with the economic aspect of a man's professional choice – to put it bluntly, the question of his income – is, if I may say so, a sign of the masculinity of the critic; it certainly bypasses the feminine quality of Austen's realism.
>
> Because . . . she saw the only act of choice in a woman's life as the making of a marriage upon which alone depended her spiritual and physical health, Austen turned a severe and serious eye (for here she was rarely satirical) on the economic life of her heroes.
>
> (Moers 1978: 70–1)

Starting to put together lost and marginalised traditions of women's relation to writing, we inevitably arrive at the women who were left out, whose books went out of print, often surprisingly quickly. Women like Jean Rhys, who caused a minor sensation in the 1960s by being not just alive when presumed dead, but also still writing. Women like Winifred Holtby, a tireless campaigner for women's rights, journalist and novelist.

A seemingly endless stream of women, brought back into culture through a strategy of re-publication and promotion. Virago Press has led the way in this country with its extensive list, currently over 200 titles of Virago Modern Classics. Distinctive presentation, coupled with scholarly introductions, have assured them a popular turnover, essential reading on any number of Women's Studies Courses and a following amongst a more broadly-based women's reading public.

This work has both enabled and is the product of the resurgence in feminist literary studies. It is a tremendous achievement and not to be decried. However, the work of reclaiming women's writing history has sometimes led to uneasy compromises with the politics of the present moment. Sometimes the simple fact of female authorship does not warrant the recirculation of work. That each book comes with a contextualising introduction and in many cases is going to be read in an educational context is good. What would be better, would be for Virago also to support a critical project: commissioning and publishing works of commentary, interpretation and literary history. The connection between books, authors and literary periods would benefit from study, as would a clearer sense of the rationale behind some decisions to republish.

There are also questions about which books are still excluded from print. Inevitably this draws out the issues of class and race, as they concern women. It took a long time before the Black American heritage of women writers, in the writing of Ann Petry and Zora Neale Hurston broke through. Working-class writers have overall been badly served in the reprint game, something which compounds the disadvantage they originally wrote from. The mosaic of feminist publishing shows some odd gaps and joins. Some given by the original distorting pressures upon women's lives; others there because bias and prejudice filter into the present, shaping and determining our sense of the literary world's composition and past. How, for example, to explain the absence of lesbian classics?

When feminist reprints first began, the category of women was sufficient. It was original and the focus of a struggle within patriarchy against sexism. The complexity of the term 'women' and the often conflicting political identities and struggles it carried in its wake came later. Nowadays the word 'women' is barely able to work as a defining, or organising concept. This is a healthy and progressive state of affairs, to be thinking always of the particular and specific. At the same time, within literature as a set of market relations, women have become hot property. In publishing terms, the tag 'Women's' sells books, so there has been a capitalisation upon this, sometimes to the benefit of feminism, other times not.

The category of women has been modified, diversified: the categories it becomes reordered into are not always given by the politics of feminism nor the organisation of the literary forms available to women writers. Thus we have Pandora Women Crime Writers and Virago Travellers; Irish and Scottish Classics, Pandora's

Mothers of the Novel. Why don't we have Lesbian Classics? Why don't we have Working-Class or Socialist Classics? Anti-Racist or Heritage Classics? Because there is no market for them, perhaps, or because the market there is does not command sufficient economic or cultural power to warrant risking the negative associations these categories can generate. It seems no coincidence that Sheba, a feminist press which has consistently prioritised writing by lesbians, working-class women and women of colour, has been less successful commercially, always in independent ownership and subjected to campaigns of vilification by the popular press, all of which are in marked contrast to the fortunes of the other feminist presses.

COURSES

Reputations and realities

This was the first course we organised which was entirely histori-cally based. It was devised in co-operation with a previous group, who were confident readers and eager to develop the range of their reading. Students were encouraged to read at least one novel or short story by the authors we were studying. Most of the sessions involved a fairly detailed talk on a general topic, lasting about thirty to forty-five minutes, followed by discussion. We included some close work on handouts which were given out during the session to give the students a more active role.

The course looked at a literary period, the 1920s and 1930s, from the perspective of women's writing and in particular Virginia Woolf, Katherine Mansfield and Winifred Holtby, whose subse-quent reputations were examined. We were inspired by our own passion for the writers and guided by Adrienne Rich's obser-vations:

> One serious cultural obstacle encountered by any feminist writer is that each feminist work has tended to be received as if it emerged from nowhere; as if each of us had lived, thought and worked without any historical past or contextual present.
>
> (Rich 1980: 11)

Our key concept for the course was re-evaluation: to ask what people – students, critics, educationalists, biographers – thought about these writers and why. Each author had a very distinct and, we felt, partial literary reputation. Winifred Holtby needed to be brought out from the shadow of Vera Brittain, Katherine Mansfield needed to lose the twin stigmas of sexual precocity and consumptive frailty, and Virginia Woolf's predominant reputation of indulgent individualism and constant neurosis needed to be reconsidered.

The first session was entitled: 'What images do we have of these writers, and where do they come from?'

It had three aims which were:

1 To see why everyone had come; why they had picked this course and what expectations they had.
2 To discover how much students already knew or had read about the authors and around the subject.
3 To discuss why we had chosen these particular writers; to see what significance they have and what they represent; to compare the images we have of them, and see how realistic these views might be and to discuss where these images have come from and whether they distort our view.

Students' reasons for attending were various. Some came because they knew a little about one of the authors, usually Virginia Woolf, and wanted to know more; others because they had enjoyed previous courses.

The second session gave a history of the period. We again started by pooling their images and understandings and then worked forwards to fill in details about prevailing ideas, political issues and social life. The third session introduced Winifred Holtby and discussed her final novel, *South Riding*. The fourth session introduced Katherine Mansfield, looking at her story *The Daughters of the Late Colonel*, the fifth, Virginia Woolf and her novel *The Years*. We then had two general sessions, the sixth on the literary critical reputations of the authors and the seventh on the literary profession for women. The eighth session looked at Virginia Woolf's novel *Mrs Dalloway* and we concluded by looking at the various letters and journals left by the three writers.

In the first session, we asked students to say the first thing that came into their head when we said each of the author's names. Not surprisingly, there was most to say about Virginia Woolf. Virtually no one had heard of Winifred Holtby and the only association made with her was Yorkshire. Students recognised the name Katherine Mansfield, but not very many women had read her work. The impression students had was that she was genteel and associated with sunshine. Virginia Woolf's list was as follows: snobbish, Bloomsbury, madness, suicide, hated Katherine Mansfield, pacifist, childless and difficult to understand.

We then asked how these writers were visualised, an interesting question which most people had difficulty with. It was as if writers were their books, disembodied and quite detached from any notion of real women. We then passed around a series of photographs, chosen for their variety: for example, Virginia Woolf laughing, Winifred Holtby in fancy dress, the women on their own and in company. How did the photographic images compare with the prevailing impressions we had just discussed?

The ensuing discussion touched on the following points, often introduced through a question or observation one of us introduced. Why has there been so much work on Virginia Woolf and comparatively little on Winifred Holtby and Katherine Mansfield? What differences, if any, had the contemporary women's liberation movement contributed? First encounters with the writers and what, if anything, was known of their lives? Is it possible to write a factual or objective biography? Did knowing, or not knowing, about the writers' lives affect how the writing was approached? What happens to a writer's life when it becomes public property? What sort of connections between the writers were known? How do we, as sympathisers or active feminists, regard women writers who are not avowedly feminist?

The image students had of the period between the First and Second World Wars was a contradictory one. On the one hand it signified unemployment and poverty, on the other, glamour and ostentatious living. We were concerned to show how those images co-existed, and the uses they were put to in the present political climate. We also attempted to show how many different versions of 'The Thirties' there were, depending on factors such as class, region, and sex. So, for instance we pointed out how the traditional images of poverty and hardship associated with the 1930s were relevant only in certain parts of the country, those concerned with manufacture and other staple industry, whereas for other areas, notably the Midlands and the South East, the interwar period was a time of expansion.

The account of the period we gave students was primarily a political and economic one, sketching out the boundaries of social and cultural life as they could be determined through legislation, electoral change and major public events such as the 1926 General Strike, 1929 Wall Street Crash, 1931 introduction of the Means Test, 1936 Spanish Civil War, 1937 establishment of the Irish Republic and so on. We also drew out the particular history of women, especially the changing patterns of employment, the impact of granting full suffrage rights in 1928 and the consequences of significant numbers of women remaining unmarried. This rise in the number of single women, and their consequent involvement in social life and political struggle, whether as feminists or not, was often not a question of choice and could be traced back to the devastating losses of the 1914–18 war. For other women, the situation was welcomed as the culmination of decades of struggle for women's independence.

Class divisions were at their most visible and critical throughout this period, and were particularly acute where women were concerned. This was the last time that domestic service prevailed and even the most modest of middle-class households employed at least one servant. All the leading feminist activists of this period, with the exception of the leading women trade unionists, employed servants, usually a maid, a cook and a cleaner, and they often lived in. The women benefiting from feminist organising and struggle, were assumed to be middle-class. Working-class women's concerns were often ignored. If they were taken up, it was often thoughtlessly. A prominent campaign which divided women in this way concerned protection of employment. Middle-class women sought to restrict the employment of women on grounds of their welfare, which working-class women interpreted as interference with their right, and necessity, to earn money.

Where class interests crossed more constructively was in the various campaigns around health and welfare which ran throughout the period. Many of these were administered or propagandised through the Co-operative Women's Guild, an organisation which was led by middle-class women but which also created opportunities for many working-class women. The Labour Party, too, during this period put great emphasis on motherhood, seeing it as an iconic symbol which would galvanise social welfare and progress. While this had the disadvantage of condensing issues to do with women to issues to do with mothers, and also fixing an image of the mother as semi-hallowed victim, it also enabled concern about infant and maternal mortality rates to be voiced in the public arena, through

113

the activity and reports of investigative committees. Significant change was not always possible however. Infant mortality rates fell throughout the period, but the maternal mortality rate increased and there are documented accounts of women literally starving to death. Mrs Minnie Weaving, for example, who died in 1933 was the subject of a coroner's inquest (Alan Hutt's *The Conditions of the Working Class in Britain*, 1933).

The glamour of the period, and its association with sexual freedom, was shown to be restricted to the upper classes. Often frivolous, the period did also give rise to more serious sexual radicals, notably Dora Russell, and the publication in English of Freud, by the Hogarth Press, led to an interest in the unconscious and questions of sexual behaviour, morality and influence.

The background talk acted as a reference for future sessions, encouraging students to question how far the works they were reading reflected these major social changes in the experience and expectations of women.

In approaching the writing itself we aimed to provide women with the opportunity to:

1 Read and discuss extracts from novels or complete short stories by the three writers.
2 Present an account of their writing lives and critical reputations, paying particular attention to whether this had changed at all and for what reasons.
3 Provide a guide to further reading.

We began with Winifred Holtby, whose writing is more immediately accessible, although she herself is less well known than Katherine Mansfield or Virginia Woolf. As an introduction, we gave students two biographical summaries: one from the 1981 Fontana edition of Vera Brittain's *Testament of Friendship* and the other from the Virago edition, that same year, of *A Crowded Street*. Directing attention to how the writer has been represented is useful on two counts. It is a convenient way of presenting biographical details and also raises issues about how that information was selected and organised. We followed this method with both Virginia Woolf and Katherine Mansfield. With Winifred Holtby, there was very little difference in emphasis. Virago rounded out the facts of her working life as a journalist and author with more detail, and included references to Winifred Holtby's work for The League of Nations Union. They also gave a complete list of her books, including *Women in a Changing Civilization*, whereas Fontana just referred to 'works of non-fiction and several novels'.

Our presentation of Winifred Holtby was concerned to acknowledge the centrality of her relationship with Vera Brittain, but at the same time to free Winifred Holtby from it. With the successful TV serialisation of *Testament of Youth*, followed by the republication in a mass paperback edition of both that novel and *Testament of Friendship*, Winifred Holtby was perceived as subordinate to, and of less significance than, Vera Brittain. This was an ironic commentary on their actual life together, because Winifred had been far more successful in the partnership, something which at times caused difficulties for Vera. At the same time, it left out the range of political campaigns which Winifred Holtby had worked for, especially her commitment to the cause of Black freedom in South Africa.

Winifred Holtby's feminism, which was largely expressed through her work with the 6 Point Group, a campaigning educational organisation linked to women's new responsibility as voters, was never the sole characteristic of her politics. Her commitment to equality embraced women, international issues and, centrally, peace. Not uncommonly for feminists at that time, her politics did not easily include issues of class and where they did, it was less the self-advocacy of working–class women that interested her than opportunities for them to move out of their class, primarily through education. From a distance of fifty years, which makes this seem misguided and patronising, it is sobering to compare it with much feminism of the time which assumed working-class women would continue to manage the domestic lives of middle-class women now free to participate in the public sphere.

Journalism and lecturing was the main work of Winifred Holtby's life. She worked for a number of influential magazines and papers, including *Time and Tide* and the *Manchester Guardian*. Her death at the early age of thirty-seven was no doubt precipitated by overwork, as in addition to her journalism she travelled widely in connection with her campaigns for peace and also wrote seven novels and a number of non-fiction works, including a critical study of Virginia Woolf. The novels are themselves varied, reflecting the different facets of her political concerns, but their emphasis lies with women. She was held in high esteem during her life, both as a novelist and activist, but her reputation faded into obscurity in the post-war years.

South Riding, published posthumously in 1937, is her most famous work and in many ways it encapsulates her main preoccupations as a writer and campaigner. It was this novel which we asked the class to read and discuss over the coming weeks, bearing in mind a number of questions.

1 What would you say this novel is about?
  Does it have any relevance today?
2 List as many things as you can which indicate that the novel was written fifty years ago.
  Think about attitudes as well as everyday life.
3 What does the novel tell you about women's lives in the 1930s?
4 Who are the main women characters in the novel and how do they differ?
  What is the purpose of the conflict between them?
5 What does the novel tell you about intimate relationships in women's lives?
6 Given what you know of Winifred Holtby's life, is this the sort of novel you would expect her to write?
7 Has reading *South Riding* encouraged you to read more of her work?

Our approach to Katherine Mansfield and Virginia Woolf differed because both writers had substantial literary reputations and had attracted a considerable amount of biographical and critical attention. As well as exploring the nature of this critical work, we also wanted to put them into context as writers from that particular historical period and challenge the notion that 'great writing' floated above considerations of time and place.

Katherine Mansfield has had far more biographical than critical attention, partly because she wrote short stories, a form which has an uneasy status within the literary establishment. We looked at *The Life of Katherine Mansfield* by Anthony Alpers (1980) and *Katherine Mansfield* by Jeffrey Meyers (1978), comparing their approach and noting that they were both overly concerned with John Middleton Murry, Katherine Mansfield's husband. Alpers was biased in his favour, Meyers against. We also referred to *Katherine Mansfield: The Memories of LM* by LM (1985). Our account began by acknowledging the problems Katherine Mansfield posed: she was not a feminist, treated people, including LM, badly and her general lack of sympathy as a character is only partially mitigated by her ill-health. Her body of work is small and her authorial presence minimal. Nevertheless, none of this excuses the way she is treated by her male biographers, who fail to take her seriously as a woman or a writer. It was about ten years later that Claire Tomalin's thoughtful reassessment appeared to counter this.

Both Alpers and Meyers accept John Middleton Murry's account of Katherine and their life together. In his version, her criticisms of him are erased and her reality disappears in the myth he creates of her as fey and childlike, dependent upon his guidance to write. Her biographers pick up and extend this, so that in their accounts Katherine Mansfield appears wilful, promiscuous, immature and deceitful, in general lacking control. Meyers, for example, glibly talks about Mansfield's 'emotional instability', claims she seduced Murry (on his word) and describes her as 'hard, tough, defensive and embittered'. Neither (male) author has any compunction about invading the mind of his (female) subject.

Reading each biography, it became clear how irrelevant our interests as women interested in another woman writing are to Alpers and Meyers. They appropriate the women and admonish them almost for existing, perpetuate stereotypes and indulge themselves in moral judgements about their character, behaviour and appearance. 'The little monkey', comments Alpers at one point, raising questions about why men write biographies of women and what it is they seek to illuminate. They told us far more about attitudes to writing women than about how Katherine Mansfield lived and worked as a writing woman. For that we have to turn to her own account, in letters and journals, of working out her own philosophy of writing, encapsulated in the quotation, 'The defeat of the personal'.

It was this, rather than the lurid and distorted views of her personality, that we encouraged students to bring to bear on her writing. For each of the stories we read, we asked:

What does 'the defeat of the personal' imply here?
How does this intention break with the past?
What philosophical or political connotations does it have?

We read 'At The Bay' and 'Daughters of the Late Colonel'. Our concern was with how families were represented in the stories: what they were and what they mean. We also spent some time discussing the ways she wrote about children. Through the journal and letters, Katherine Mansfield's commitment to the craft of writing is evident. We compared half a dozen of her opening lines, noting how they convey the impression of something having already happened, creating the impression that they stop time rather than recreate it. Part of the pleasure, too, of Katherine Mansfield's writing is that it looks very easy. After spending some time analysing her style, we asked students to write a story imitating her style. This was a challenging exercise, which most of us couldn't complete, but which taught us a great deal.

People had most preconceptions about Virginia Woolf and they were largely negative. Our approach involved three distinct strands. We looked at the changes in how Virginia Woolf's work had been considered by different generations of critics. We looked at how Virginia Woolf herself viewed her writing and finally, as it plays such a significant part in attitudes towards her, and other women writers, we looked at madness.

The critical interest began with Winifred Holtby's study of Woolf, which concentrated on the poetic and symbolic aspects of her writing. She then quickly became associated with the other exponents of modernism and writing as a stream of conscious-ness. Linked with writers such as James Joyce, Marcel Proust and Dorothy Richardson, Virginia Woolf has always attracted serious consideration from French critics and writers, but in Britain she became associated, as did other modernists, with long books which were difficult to read. In Britain, her reputation was formed partly through the baleful influence of the Leavises and the writers associated with *Scrutiny*, who dominated the teaching of English throughout the school system well into the 1960s.

Virginia Woolf was seen in the context of Bloomsbury. An image of the Bloomsbury set as snobbish, elitist, intellectual aesthetes hardened over the years. Throughout the late 1950s and 1960s the image itself remained unchallenged, what did change was the sense of it as a good or a bad thing. As *Scrutiny* came under attack, modernism was reassessed, as was the importance of the Bloomsbury group, notably in J. K. Johnstone's serious reappraisal. Even so, Virginia Woolf's writing kept its reputation for being difficult in a way that others did not.

After the publication of *Portrait of a Marriage* and with the gradual publication of the letters and diaries, a more rounded view of Virginia Woolf started to emerge. But, as a more human account developed so too did the stress on her periods of madness and depression. After 1972, when criticism itself diverged in many directions, Virginia Woolf's writing was dissected from a number of different points of interest: androgyny; character interpretation; formalist; marxist; feminist; structuralist. The range of her writing – the fiction and non-fiction, the letters and diaries – only slowly emerged and the differences between her writing are so great that it is possible for theories about her writing to be erected on the basis of an only partial reading of her work. For example, a reading of *The Common Reader, Orlando* and *A Room Of One's Own* give particular and one-sided images of her work and do not necessarily prepare a reader for the rest of her writing.

The novels we read together were *The Years* and *Mrs Dalloway*. We outlined an approach to reading through a series of questions which led to discussion about reading in general and Virginia Woolf in particular. These were:

1 What do we look for in a novel? What are the implications of this *re:* feminist/women's writing?
2 How much are we aware of the design/form of a novel as we read it?
3 How does this relate to our experience of reading and what we choose to read?
4 What was Virginia Woolf trying to do in her novels?
5 How did she write her novels?
6 How does Virginia Woolf's non-fiction fit with this?
7 How does what she was trying to do and what she wrote relate to a feminist perspective, then and now? How and why do we read Virginia Woolf today and are there any problems?

In addition to these questions, we gave students a handout which summarised Virginia Woolf's writing career and quoted from her letters and diaries from 1915 onwards, when *The Voyage Out* was published. We selected points where she talked directly about herself as a writer.

We looked at *Mrs Dalloway* with an additional set of questions derived from issues to do with women, writing and madness. Our first question was: 'What is women's madness?' and we explored it by considering the ways in which women's lives and sexuality are pathologised and the difficulties which stand in the way of women achieving a positive sense of self. The relationship between depression, anger and madness was also discussed, especially in relation to a double standard which upholds and valorises feminine ideals in behaviour and yet imposes taboos on the physical and emotional realities of women's lives: menstruation, childbirth and menopause. Our second question was: 'What do women do with their madness?', our third: 'What does society do with women's madness and/or anger?'

We approached *Mrs Dalloway* not as a book about madness, but as one about alienation, isolation, sense and security of self. The central question it poses is: to what extent is security of self derived from other people? The characters of Septimus and Clarissa represent two different sides to madness. Clarissa is withdrawn and in retreat, depressive, isolated and alienated. Septimus on the other hand, while also isolated, is manic: looking for and imagining breakthroughs into new knowledges. Although they can be seen as two aspects of the same personality, as attempts to explore the complexity and completeness of madness, there is an inequality between them. War produced, and thus excuses, the dislocation and dissolution that is Septimus's madness whereas Clarissa has no excuse at all. The symbol of a party that Virginia Woolf uses to represent wholeness and communication is not entirely adequate, excluding as it does the world of work and restricting itself to a very limited social group.

By the end of the course, students had read a range of texts by and about the three writers and discussed them in relation to each other as well as in a more general context of women's writing in the inter-war period. In the process they had gained the confidence to approach unfamiliar and apparently difficult or unrewarding texts. The value of this in their further reading of works by Katherine Mansfield, Virginia Woolf or Winifred Holtby was clear. What also became apparent was that these skills could be transferred to other reading situations.

LESBIAN WRITING

Historical approaches to writing are often, as with Reputations and Realities, a case of going back to standard literary texts and examining them in new contexts or with new questions. In some instances, though, looking back to history is a radical and empowering activity that rarely involves dealing with the traditional literary past.

Social groups that experience cultural silencing or subordination are often also denied access to the main cultural outlets too, even though they may have their own thriving traditions of cultural achievement. Black American writers from the Harlem Renaissance of the 1920s onwards have only survived patchily into the present day; lesbian writing has an oblique and obscured continuity through time. Everything that is true of women's history and women's dispossession from their pasts becomes keener when the women in question are of a subordinate race and/or lesbians.

Although examining the nature of lesbian existence is always present in lesbian writing, other topics are explored too. It is important when putting together any course that the most is made of opportunities to represent lesbian writing about, for example, motherhood or work. However, such a pluralist approach rarely enables students, whether lesbian or not, to get to grips with the nature of lesbian writing as a distinct and different relation to writing and publishing and to understand its relation to lesbian life.

Historical approaches are crucial to that understanding, enabling as they do the recognition of lesbianism's continuity, thus challenging attitudes which regard it as either a product of contemporary permissiveness or a phase in an individual woman's life which should be grown out of. At the same time, attention is directed towards the historical continuity of oppression lesbians have faced and the consequences of this for writing.

There are many different, sometimes conflicting, understandings of what lesbianism is, ranging from the pathological to the political. Problems of definition can be acute when considering contemporary writing, but at least there we have the writers' own sense of allegiance to weigh with our own judgements. Once we move back, even a generation or two, the difficulties multiply.

The word lesbianism is very recent, but the identity and activity to which it refers takes us back to Lesbos and Sappho in 600 BC. It would, however, be too simplistic to read back an unbroken line through from Sappho to the present day. Lesbianism is defined partly, some would argue exclusively, through the presence of an erotic relationship between women. It is difficult to lay this template on histories and cultures in which all female sexuality has been highly regulated and often explicitly controlled by and for men.

The problems this raises are compounded when lesbianism is also defined through emotional or political commitment to women in ways which decentre the erotic and sexual. Having agreed a working definition of lesbianism, or as we would recommend, bringing into the mainstream of the class discussion precisely those shifts in meaning and definition, a second set of important decisions arise. What do we mean by lesbian writing? Are we concerned with one or all of the following: writing by lesbians about lesbianism; writing about lesbianism by anyone; writing about anything by lesbians.

We would argue that a history of lesbian writing course needs to take all three into consideration, because our aim would be to explore the social construction of lesbianism and the relationship between that and individual lesbian writers and, where relevant, lesbian networks. Such philosophical difficulties are, however, often overshadowed by the practical considerations. The most significant of which is access, operating in terms both historical and contemporary. Prejudice and fear often operate in such a way that explicit records of lesbianism are either destroyed by future generations or have failed to be recorded in the first place. Where such records do exist, and writing is important to lesbians precisely because it is often the only public record of existence available to them, they can be misleading.

The biases within the culture at large which work against working-class women and women of colour, are often reproduced within lesbianism so that records of these women's lives, thoughts and feelings *as lesbians* are difficult, if not impossible, to come by. Male homosexual culture in Britain has clear cross-class dimensions to it, however exploitative these may sometimes appear, whereas lesbian lives appear to follow more rigid class divisions. There is very little documentation of the historical presence in Britain of Black lesbian and gay lives. In America, the situation differs, not least in that Lesbian Studies, including historical research, informed by a variety of class and race experiences, is much better established and consequently more extensive than here.

Uncovering a lesbian past often involves being limited to a narrower class and racial base than is desirable. In the absence of texts which document those experiences, it is important to question those generated and surviving. In doing this, part of the motive should be to dispel the notion that homosexuality is the vice of a degenerate aristocracy, and partly to give students permission to think against the grain: why should the heterosexual assumption have any more validity in the past than it does now?

Access is also relevant to those texts which were published and have survived. Lesbian writing from the past has rarely gone into popular editions which it has been considered worthwhile to keep in print. *The Well of Loneliness*, that most problematic of lesbian novels, can readily be found, but many others are now only in copyright libraries. American feminist publishers have been quicker than the British ones to reprint lesbian classics and though these books are distributed over here they are more expensive and less easy to find.

As the women's liberation movement itself discovered, changes in social attitude, educational practice and the curriculum depend upon an infrastructure of publishing, distribution and support for writers and researchers. For Lesbian Studies, this is much more fragile and has recently been undermined by the assault on civil liberty which Section 28 of the Local Government Act 1989 represents. Adult education, as a non-statutory sector, is the one most important to the development of Lesbian Studies, as it has been to Women's Studies generally. From time to time, tension around how far Women's Studies should incorporate lesbian themes and issues surfaces in acrimonious ways. We see this as a clear instance of divide and rule: if it is such a fearful thing to be associated with, or 'accused of', lesbianism, shouldn't that in itself warrant further investigation? What are the arguments against women tutors and students examining their heterosexism, who is making them, and whose interests do they serve?

Suggested course outline

Aims

To establish that lesbianism and lesbian writing has a past.
To introduce students to writing and writers they may be unfamiliar with.
To generate discussion about the status and value of a lesbian tradition in writing.

Session 1

Introduction to the course, each other and ways of working.
Ask students to go round saying their name and the first lesbian book they read.
Have prepared a sheet with a variety of definitions of the word lesbian: these can be drawn from different editions of dictionaries;

psychologists; sexologists; feminist and lesbian political theorists. Try to get a spread of types of description/definition and of dates. Ask students to discuss in groups of three, with a few guiding questions, e.g.: Are you uncomfortable with any of these? Why? How has the meaning of the word 'lesbian' changed? What do you think is responsible for that?

Round table discussion to establish how many lesbians, writers or not, from the past the group can come up with. Encourage people to think about how they found out what they know. If it is a small list, put together with difficulty, ask people to concentrate on why they think that is so.

Session 2

Divide the group into threes and ask them to discuss and then report back on their reading history as lesbians using these questions:

1 What were the first lesbian books you read?
2 How did you find out about them?
3 What do you think about them now?
4 In what way is reading important to you?
5 What was the last lesbian book you recommended and why?
6 What are you looking for in writing by lesbians?

Session 3 onwards

In subsequent sessions, we discussed extracts given a week in advance. We introduced each week with a summary of points from the previous week and with a short introduction contextualising the pieces selected. The topics we covered were:

Radclyffe Hall

Extracts: *The Well of Loneliness* and *The Unlit Lamp*.
The introduction covered her biography, the obscenity trial and summarised the books.
The questions were:

1 What is the value of reading these books now?
2 What version of lesbian identity do they give?

3 In what ways is it useful to read *The Unlit Lamp* as a novel about lesbianism?

Paris between the Wars

Extracts: *The Ladies' Almanack* Djuna Barnes; *Claudine Married* Colette; *Lifting Belly* Gertrude Stein; and *A Woman Appeared to Me* Renée Vivien. The introduction covered their biographies, discussed modernism and the attractions it had for some lesbian writers and referred to the other lesbian writers and artists in Paris at that time who we were not covering.

1 How enjoyable are these pieces?
2 How easy to understand?
3 Does modernism obscure questions of lesbianism?

Bloomsbury

Extracts: *The Letters of Virginia Woolf and Vita Sackville-West*; *Orlando* Virginia Woolf; *Portrait of a Marriage* Nigel Nicolson; *Letters between Vita Sackville-West and Violet Trefusis*; *Olivia*, Olivia.
The introduction provided a guide to Bloomsbury, noting the ways in which the dominant views – either partisan or derisory – were partial and discussed the role of biographers in creating, and at times distorting, public figures.
How do we deal with sexual ambiguity in terms of lesbian writing?

The twilight zone

Extracts: *Beebo Brinker* Anne Bannon; *Loving Her* Anne Allen Shockley; *The Microcosm* Maureen Duffy and *The Price of Salt* Claire Morgan.
The introduction pointed out how tongue-in-cheek the title was, although it was a real quote from a dust jacket in the 1960s, which went on to refer to lesbianism as 'the tragic trivial'. We then talked about lesbian life, and writing, in the 1950s and 1960s before introducing the books.

1 Have things changed?
2 Why do we like these books?
3 What makes us uncomfortable about them?

Feminism's impact

Extracts (focused on taking initiatives and attraction between women): *Cactus* Anna Wilson and *Rubyfruit Jungle* Rita Mae Brown. The introduction summarised these books and talked about their reception when first published.

What difference does feminism make?

Class and race

Extracts: *Brainchild* Eve Croft; *Three Ply Yarn* Caeiae March; *Falling* Barbara Burford.

The introduction talked about the kinds of assumptions made about what sort of women are lesbians, and the hidden histories within lesbian history of Black and working-class women's experience.

What difference does class and race make?

Autobiography

Extracts: *Zami* Audre Lorde and *Corridor of Mirrors* Rosemary Manning.

The introduction talked about the importance of autobiography, given how few lesbian biographies are written. Their potential to link self development with social processes and explore the tension between individuality and typicality were touched on. The range of autobiographies was briefly indicated.

Compare and contrast the two extracts.

Contemporary questions

Extracts: Introductions from *The Reach* and *Girls Next Door*, which both spoke of a 'coming of age' in lesbian writing. This involved no longer needing to write the coming out story, but being able to write the many and varied being out stories that make up lesbian existence.

Do you agree with these points?

This format was designed, and works well, as an introductory session. There is a lot of potential for follow-on courses, going into more detail and tackling specific forms, such as poetry or drama, which were not covered here. It is also possible to take a theme, such as autobiographical writing, and cover that in detail.

Women, war and peace

The mobilisation of women against nuclear weapons, specifically at Greenham Common during the early 1980s, is just the latest example of a complicated relationship which women have to war, that most masculine of activities, and peace. As such, it provides a valuable basis for a course to break the stereotypical identification of women's interests with those of the personal, inner spaces.

Aims

1 Explore the ways women participate in and write about war.
2 Provide historical contexts for contemporary peace movements.
3 Discuss whether the themes of war and peace are imaginatively valuable for women writers.

Session 1

Introduction to course, each other and ways of working.
Ask the group to go round saying what relevance any wars had to their lives and families.
Overview from tutor which sets out and takes issue with the popular conception that women writers have avoided issues of the wider world and war. Reference could be made, for instance, to the plots of *Shirley* by Charlotte Brontë and *Persuasion* by Jane Austen, which both draw on a knowledge of war, as well as more recent writing.

Sessions 2 and 3

Ministering Angels?

Extracts: *Biography/Letters of Florence Nightingale*; *The Wonderful Adventures of Mrs Seacole* ed. Ziggy Alexander; *Testament of Youth* Vera Brittain and *Step-Daughters of War* Helen Smith.

1 To what extent was war liberating for women?

2 What are the implications for women of their nursing role during war?
3 What other roles does war proscribe for women (spies, civilians, victims, collaborators, prostitutes)? How and by whom do these get written about?

Sessions 4 and 5

Joining up

Extracts: *Aye, Aye Nelson* Nancy Spain; *All Those Brave Promises* Dorothy Lee Settle; *Does Khaki Become You?* Cynthia Enloe

1 Do women join up during wars for different reasons than in peace time?
2 What are the forms of disillusion with service life?
3 Have you ever considered, or joined, the forces; When and why?

Sessions 6 and 7

Fighting for peace

Extracts: *Militarism versus Feminism* Mary Sargent Florence; *Breaching the Peace* Catherine Marshall & C. K. Ogden; Alice Walker, essay in *Home Girls*; 'Is Violence Masculine? A Black Feminist Perspective' Kum Kum Bhavnani in *Charting the Journey*.

1 What comparisons can you draw between the various twentieth-century women's peace movements?
2 Do you see any difficulties in identifying women with pacificism?

Sessions 8 and 9

Just wars?

Extracts: *The Diary of Anne Frank*; *The Way-Paver* Anne Devlin; *My Life* Ellen Kuzwayo; *No Mate for the Magpie* Frances Molloy; *Requiem* Shuziko Go; *Frost in the Morning* Janine Baum.

1 Can objections to war be overridden by the pressure of particular and immediate circumstances?

2 How can women resist in times of war?

Session 10

Mud by Nicky Edwards

1 How are the differences between nuclear and conventional warfare treated?
2 Does the novel communicate why women took the actions they did at Greenham and other Peace Camps?
3 Is Jo's exhaustion plausible?
4 In what ways does the novel affirm or challenge the peace movement?

Session 11

The Burning Book by Maggie Gee

1 Is this a novel about war or peace?
2 What are the sources of its power: propaganda, emotion, imagination?
3 Is it in any way distinctively a woman's book?

Session 12

Conclusions

Divide the group into pairs to work through these questions, then pool responses in a general discussion.

1 What has been the most valuable aspect of this course?
2 Has it challenged any of your thinking about women, war and peace?
3 Do you think women write about war differently from men?
4 Is there anything you now feel more confused about?
5 Does this feel positive or not?
6 What are you going to do about it?

5

POETRY: PROBLEMS AND PLEASURES

Poetry has the curious status of being simultaneously the most accessible and the most excluding of literary forms. In teaching, it is the exclusions that tend to dominate. 'No poetry' is the commonest request we get when negotiating course content in our Return to Learning classes. Undoubtedly, poetry puts people off. In this section we argue that it doesn't have to, and offer some examples of how to teach with and about poetry to students who see it as pointless, too difficult, or nothing to do with them.

Students are not the only ones who have trouble with poetry. Often it is the tutor's own internalisation of the study of poetry as too complex, demanding its own specialised critical language, that keeps it outside the classroom door. Or, as was the case with us, a reluctance to bring into the classroom the one area of literature that we did not feel obliged to interpret, introduce or teach to others.

Women have always written poetry, just as they have always had to battle for their work to be taken seriously. The traditions of women poets are much less accessible than those of their sister novelists. If we are to believe the critics, women write rhymes and verse, their claims to the title of poet ridiculed by the label 'poetess'. For tutors, brought up on the biases of our literary education, teaching poetry often hasn't arisen as an option, so powerfully has it seemed to be teaching the writing of men. The last fifteen years have seen an enormous expansion not just in the numbers of women poets publishing and performing their work, but also in scholarship that has begun to trace the traditions of women's relation to poetical language and generate a new critical enquiry into women poets. Significant writers here include Louise Bernikow, Alicia Suskin Ostriker, Janet Montefiore and Judy Grahn. Feminist and Black politics took poetry into the heart of their struggles to challenge, educate and move people. For Black poets in particular, the move to poetry had less to do with academic literary culture than with a return to the egalitarian, oral roots of poetry.

With these changes, and the inspirational, entertaining and powerful work of poets as diverse as Judy Grahn, Adrienne Rich, Marge Piercy, Merle Collins, Jackie Kay, Michèle Roberts and Alison Fell, we found it impossible to avoid bringing poetry into our teaching. Initially, we allocated one or two sessions in a course to poetry, or used individual poems to illustrate themes under discussion. Knowing how to present the poems, especially to students in Basic Education classes, posed some problems to begin with. However, we felt that poetry was, at one level, just another form of writing and that any tutor working to develop reading, writing and comprehension skills in her students should be providing them with as wide a range of material as possible. Also, the way in which poetry encapsulates ideas and emotions in imagery and symbols was not dissimilar to the massive complexities of symbolism utilised in advertising, which does not require functional literacy in order to be understood.

Poetry is used both as a means of conveying ideas and evoking emotions, and as another way of speaking. It was these ideas that we wanted to develop when we used Marge Piercy's *What's That Smell in the Kitchen?* (Piercy 1983: 20) as the basis of a lesson with a women's literacy group, none of whom had 'studied' poetry or had any formal educational qualifications. Many had little habit of reading beyond the newspaper, and lacked confidence in their ability to comprehend complex ideas on paper, though they were all skilled in discussion.

Usually in a literacy class students read aloud, discussing the meaning of words as we go along. With poetry, the tutor should read the piece first to give students an opportunity to experience the sounds and rhythms. This is particularly important because a poem does not necessarily tell a story and is not always a straightforward piece of narrative; it also provides students with space to concentrate on listening without having to worry too much about their own ability to read and follow all the words accurately. Before reading, give out any information you have about the author or context. After an initial reading, ask if the women would like to hear it again, which they usually would. Then ask if there were any words or expressions that were unfamiliar, and also what they thought the poem was about. In Marge Piercy's poem the names of American towns and words like *insomniac* were cited; we looked at the atlas to find the towns, and group members were able to supply meanings for insomniac. At this stage most of the women had picked up on the cooking imagery, and some identified the husband as a character within the poem.

One of the most important things to remember when working with poetry in any group is that the tutor, whatever her own background and critical skills, is privileged by having read and thought about the poem prior to the lesson. Poetry does not always come straight to the point; frequently there is not a discernible point to come to. One understands a poem by reading and re-reading, and it is this process that you re-enact in the class situation, bearing always in mind that although you may have already done this, your students have not. Their own attitudes towards poetry – as something difficult, airy-fairy, boring and specialised – are compounded in the case of the students with reading difficulties by a lifetime of being bewildered, intimidated and made to feel inadequate by the written word. Hence the importance of reading aloud.

After the initial readings and discussions about unfamiliar words, ask the group to read the poem aloud to themselves. Do this by going round the group, asking each woman to read a short passage. For instance, we might break at '. . . beans in Dallas', '. . . glittering like wax', '. . . the back of her eyes', '. . . heart of an insomniac', '. . . but now I am Spam', '. . . but war'. The placing of the breaks depends on the abilities of the women concerned and the number of women in the group. As each woman reads it will be clear to the tutor whether there are words she has difficulty with, and to some extent her comprehension will be indicated by the fluency with which she reads. At each break, ask questions about what has been read, for example, 'What is tofu?', 'What does she mean by "calico smile"?', 'What is a clinker?' and so on. Obviously this breaks up the flow of the poem; it does, however, enable the women in the group both to experience reading the poem for themselves, and to comprehend word for word what the author is saying, and is not a process that should be rushed. For example, the 'calico smile' led to a long discussion about calico and rag dolls, which in turn gave rise to questioning about why the poet was using the image of dolls and what that meant in terms of women. Having reached the end of the poem, and checked that it was generally clear in terms of vocabulary, the group then reread it with much more fluency and familiarity.

We then took a short break, during which conversation, not surprisingly, was about cooking and about food being burned and how various women's husbands, boyfriends and sons responded to food and cooking, what they would and wouldn't eat, and how competent or otherwise they were when it came to cooking for themselves. There was some discussion about learning to cook from mothers, grandmothers and aunts, with the tutors pushing a little as to whether boys learned to cook and why were all the famous chefs men? (It was generally felt they'd probably learned from women.) It was thus easy to return to the subject matter of the poem.

At this stage of elucidation there is a two-fold concern: what is the poet saying, and how is she saying it? Direct the group to look at the last line: 'Burning dinner is not incompetence but war' – ask questions like, 'What does she mean by this?' 'Why does she use a word like war?' 'Who is the war against?' and so on. There were two views as to the deliberateness of the burning; some women felt that there were women who just weren't very good at cooking, while others discerned a sense of purpose behind the apparent incompetence. We then went through the poem again from the beginning, digressing briefly into regional foods and gradually working our way through the different types of cooking to the 'husband spitted over a slow fire'. This, and the 'dead rat with a bomb in the belly' caused some shock and dismay but by this stage everyone had firmly grasped the author's purpose, so the shock may have been occasioned either by the violence of the imagery or the extremity of the solution. The two lines 'Look, she says . . . now I am Spam' were interpreted according to various women's sense of what was glamorous and what was mundane in the way of food.

Finally, we asked why the group thought the poet had used the particular example of cooking and what she'd done with it, which led to an extended discussion of expectations within marriage and relationships, and also other ways in which women, performing their traditional roles might subvert marriage (not cleaning, burning clothes when ironing, not getting up in the morning). We also asked if the group thought the meaning of the poem could have been expressed in any other way; apart from being a fairly leading question it is extremely hard to answer, but generally the women in the group thought the poem was clever and, with some help from the tutor, clear and understandable.

Writing is usually a part of most literacy classes, but is best avoided after reading poetry, partly because standard comprehension questions are not appropriate to understanding poetry, and partly because the use of a not very familiar form in reading can sometimes lead to confusion and uncertainty when it comes to writing. Besides, it can easily take the two hours of a session to elucidate a poem, and if this does involve a considerable amount of discussion, then it also involves work leading to a wider sense of language's potential. In addition to this use of poetry, theme-based courses in women's writing offer many opportunities to introduce poets and poems. In our courses on mothers and daughters, sexuality and feminism, we took these opportunities and were struck by how often women expressed surprise at enjoying and understanding the poetry we selected. Realising just how distanced from poetry most of our students felt led us to devise a course designed to de-mystify poetry for them.

The course programme was as follows:

Week 1   Introduction to the course – what poetry means to me.
Week 2   Why and how do we read poems?
Week 3   What makes a poem a poem?
Week 4   What makes a poet a poet?
Week 5   What makes a poem a good poem?

Part (ii): Questions of identity. Does reading poetry by contemporary women increase our awareness of our place in the world and women's differing experiences? Have women's ideas about poetry and what poetry is about changed in the last twenty years?

Week 6   Writing as women
Week 7   Writing as Black women
Week 8   Writing as lesbians
Week 9   Conclusions

The apparent simplicity of these questions was deceptive. As tutors, presenting the introductions and devising exercises which would engage students in active discussion and learning based on them, was some of the most challenging work we had undertaken in a long time. It meant going back to where we had started with poetry and tracing the path forward in such a way that students could see and understand how they had been turned away from it. Most of us first encounter poetry as rote learning at school, followed by the equally inflexible practical criticism which inculcates a dexterity in dismembering poetry, a reading method rarely adopted outside the classroom or exam situation. Identifying metrical patterns, image repertoires and other means of formal analysis are not, in themselves, sufficient motivation to continue a wide and detailed exploration of poetry.

In the early sessions our intentions were:

1 To provide an opportunity for the group to pool its ideas, exploring how they had arrived at those definitions.
2 To demonstrate the range of possible answers to those questions, the diversity of experience, especially cultural and/or historical difference and introduce students to as wide a range of poetry as possible.
3 To enable students to arrive at their own definitions through a process of comparison, debate and analysis.

In 'Why and How Do We Read Poems?' for example, we began by asking everyone to bring along to that session a poem that was special to them and asked them to read it to and discuss it with the group. Before that, we divided the group into pairs and asked them to work through the following questions:

1 How often do you read poetry?
2 Are you more likely to read poetry at any particular time?
3 Do you talk about that reading with anyone?
4 How did you learn to read poems?

Towards the end of the discussion that arose, we asked the group to focus on how to read a poem and they came up with guidelines which we then used for all the poems we went on to look at on the course. These involved reading a poem more than once: reading to discover what it was about, what it made us feel, how it was done; reading aloud as well as reading it over silently.

When these sessions were completed, we realised that they hadn't addressed the question of value: why we liked a particular poem or not, whether it was of value or not and how a poem could be valuable even if we personally did not like it. In order to move the discussion into this area we devised the 'Good Poem Exercise'. The use of the word 'Good' was deliberate, intended to draw students towards the word's variable uses and meanings. As the exercise proceeds, students start to ask 'What exactly do we mean by good, anyway?' and we reply, 'Exactly, what does it mean?' One of the pivots of the exercise is to show that questions of value are not absolute, they cannot be taken for granted, but also need to be interrogated and clarified.

The exercise works like this. A number of statements about what a 'Good Poem' is are set out. They should be as varied as possible, and can be amended to cover particular sorts of poetry, e.g. Black women's poetry; lesbian poetry; or depending upon the confidence and size of the group.

The statements we used included: A Good Poem is One That –

You can understand immediately
Rhymes
Needs no explanation
Can't be written any other way
Needs several readings to understand
Creates powerful new images
Means more than one thing
Lasted through time
Gives pleasure to any reader
Is above politics

Everyone has a copy and is asked to read through and respond briefly to each statement in terms of yes/no; usually/sometimes/ never. They are asked to think why they respond as they do, but the emphasis should be to get the list completed with a sense of the 'because' rather than a detailed written answer.

Then, in turn around the group the tutor asks what the answer was and why, asking each person to reply to one statement. She then asks if anyone else had a very different response or something to add. In this way, a discussion where all the group participates is built. Once all the questions have been covered and the discussion allowed to run for a while, the tutor hands out some poems.

In choosing the poems we aimed for a diversity in subject matter, tone, historical period and style. Taking the authors' names off the poems is not essential but produces some very different and interesting reactions. Where a name is known, e.g. Adrienne Rich, women will respond to what they know of the poet, tying her reputation in to their response and sometimes perhaps being inhibited, especially if they don't understand or like what the poet is doing. Poems which are not identifiable in this way produce a much more open and wide ranging set of responses, as does working at this exercise with students unfamiliar with poetry. Depending on the size and confidence of the group you can either give a poem per person or one between groups of two or three.

Poets we have chosen have included: Grace Nichols, Sylvia Plath, Denise Levertov, Adrienne Rich, Elizabeth Barrett Browning, Christina Rossetti, Emily Brontë, Anna Wickham, Emily Dickinson, Iyamide Hazeley, Olive Rogers, Marge Piercy, Stevie Smith, Sappho, Caroline Halliday, Jackie Kay, Elsa Gidlow, Judy Grahn, Charlotte Mew, Maureen Duffy, Pat Parker, Audre Lorde, Mary Dorcey, Phillis Wheatley, Radclyffe Hall.

Sometimes poems are handed out in a pot luck fashion, with the option of barter and exchange. At other times, the poems are displayed and students can choose something that appeals to them. They are asked to spend ten to fifteen minutes deciding if they think their poem is good, with reference back to the discussion and we then go round, each poem is read out and the response given. While ensuring that everyone does get a chance to make their prepared contribution, the tutor should also be letting students pick up points and respond to each other's ideas and poems.

What was so good about this exercise was that it seemed to jump all the inhibitions surrounding reading poetry out loud, talking about and responding to it. The discussion built up very easily and quickly. It was clearly very open ended. What is obvious to students very early on is that there are no right and wrong answers; the stress is on responses and starting to give reasons for them; to begin understanding and weighing any one particular response against another. Also valuable is that the discussion is so obviously cumulative, the poems chosen for their disparity, which works to diminish the self-consciousness which shows itself in group discussions either as a tendency to show off or to remain silent.

If the exercise works, students are left having experienced discussing poetry and with a range of ideas about what poetry is and having begun to situate their responses. They have also experienced reading a poem closely and examining their own and each other's reactions and opinions of it. In this very practical, text based way, the subjective and objective dimensions of responding to poetry are engaged with. The discussion moves, from student to student, student to tutor, but also from poem to poem, idea to idea. It was an excellent preparation for the more detailed work we went on to do in the sessions: Writing as a woman, Writing as a Black woman, Writing as a lesbian.

137

An exercise of this kind lays the foundation for a series of more specific approaches, perhaps based on guided questions or comprehensions which, come to cold, would have been difficult. It comes around to discussions, such as the value of rhyme, which it is difficult to imagine a group engaging with so forcefully and inquisitively had they begun with that topic alone.

The exercise explores what poems are, what is specific about them: the whole stress on language, the ways in which attention paid to language is something particular to poetry, and part of the pleasure of reading it. At the same time, a heated discussion developed about whether poetic language was, in itself, enough to make a poem valuable. Artistic preoccupations alone were not appreciated, nor was language which obscured meaning.

But meaning was allowed to be complex, in fact, as valuable as poems which were immediately accessible were those where there was a multiplicity of meaning. That complexity, which might make the expression difficult and require two or three readings before it was elucidated, had to be in the content as well as the form. There had to be a point to the poem other than its technical excellence.

The set of questions about what a good poem is, as regards form, style and language, most often produced a qualified response. Perhaps and sometimes, it can be but it doesn't have to be, was the consensus. This isn't just a vague relativism. What was being said was that how a poem is written has to be judged in a context which takes account of issues wider than poetic form.

Introducing poetry, either as the subject of a course in itself or as a means to discuss other subjects, can be difficult but the advantages are enormous. Poems are small, but complex enough for students to work closely on the text by themselves or in groups in such a way that they can achieve a sense of understanding which is much harder to experience by working on novels. The skills of analysis and comprehension developed in relation to poetry can be transferred to other learning and for other types of writing.

SELECT BIBLIOGRAPHY

ALBSU (1987) *Families*, London: ALBSU

Alexander, Z. (1988) *The Wonderful Adventures of Mrs Seacole*, Oxford: Oxford University Press

Alpers, A. (1980) *The Life of Katherine Mansfield*, London: Cape

Amiran, M. (1975) 'What Women's Literature?' in *College English*

Angelou, M. (1969) *I Know Why the Caged Bird Sings*, London: Virago

Arrowsmith, P. (1970) *Somewhere Like This*, London: Panther

Asian Women Writers Workshop (1988) *Right of Way*, London: Women's Press

Bambara, T. (1984) *Gorilla, My Love*, London: Women's Press

Bannon, A. (1986) *Beebo Brinker*, Tallahassee: Naiad

Barnes, D. (1928) *The Ladies' Almanack*, Dijon: Darantierre

Bauman, J. (1986) *Winter in the Morning*, London: Virago

Bell, Q. (1972) *Virginia Woolf*, London: Hogarth

Bennett, L. (1966) *Jamaica Labrish*, Kingston, Ja.: Sangsters

Benstock, S. (1987) *Women of the Left Bank*, London: Virago

Bernikow, L. (1979) *The World Split Open*, London: Women's Press

Bhavnani, K. (1988) 'Is Violence Masculine?' in Grewal, S. *et al.* (1988) *Charting the Journey*, London: Sheba

Bradshaw, J. and Hemmings, J. (eds) (1985) *Girls Next Door*, London: Women's Press

Brittain, V. (1981) *Testament of Friendship*, London: Fontana

Brown, R. May (1978) *Rubyfruit Jungle*, London: Corgi

Bryan, B., S. Dadzie and S. Scafe (1985) *The Heart of the Race*, London: Virago

Bulkin, E., M. B. Pratt and B. Smith (1984) *Yours in Struggle*, New York: Long Haul Press

Burford, B. (1984) *The Threshing Floor*, London: Sheba

Burford, B., G. Pearse, G. Nichols and J. Kay (n.d.) *A Dangerous Knowing*, London: Sheba

Cartledge, S. and Ryan, J. (eds) (1983) *Sex and Love: New Thoughts on Old Contradictions*, London: Women's Press

Centerprise (1984) *Breaking the Silence*, London: Centerprise

Chester, L. (1989) *Deep Down*, London: Faber

Clarke, W. (1982) 'The Dyke, the Feminist and the Devil', in *Feminist Review* 11

Cobham, R. and Collins, M. (1987) *Watchers and Seekers*, London: Women's Press

Colette (1972) *Claudine Married*, Harmondsworth: Penguin

Collins, M. (1985) *Because the Dawn Breaks*, London: Karia

Collins, M. (1987) *Angel*, London: Women's Press

Conlon, F., R. da Silva and B. Wilson (1986) *The Things that Divide Us*, London: Sheba

Cosman, C. *et al.* (1978) *Women Poets*, Harmondsworth: Penguin

Coward, R. (1982) 'Are Women's Novels Feminist Novels?' in *Feminist Review* 5

Croft, E. (n.d.) *Brainchild*, London: Onlywomen Press

Cruikshank, M. (1982) *Lesbian Studies*, New York: Feminist Press

Devlin, A. (1987) *The Way-Paver*, London: Faber

Duffy, M. (1989) *The Microcosm*, London: Virago (first published by Panther, 1967)

Edwards, N. (1986) *Mud*, London: Women's Press

Enloe, C. (1988) *Does Khaki Become You?* London: Pandora

Fairbairns, Z. (1979) *Benefits*, London: Virago

Fairbairns, Z. (ed.) (1978) *Tales I Tell My Mother*, London: Journeyman

Fell, A. (1979) *Hard Feelings*, London: Women's Press

Fell, A. (1984) *Every Move You Make*, London: Virago

Fell, A. *et al.* (1978) *Licking the Bed Clean*, London: Teeth Imprints

Fell, A. *et al.* (1980) *Smile, Smile, Smile, Smile*, London: Sheba

Feminist Review (1984) 'Many Voices, One Chant', *Feminist Review* 17

Florence, M. (1987) *Militarism versus Feminism*, London: Virago

Garcia, J. and Maitland, S. (1983) *Walking on the Water*, London: Virago

Gee, M. (1983) *The Burning Book*, London: Faber

Go, S. (1985) *Requiem*, London: Women's Press

Grahn, J. (1978) *The Work of a Common Woman*, London: Onlywomen Press

Grahn, J. (1985) *The Highest Apple* San Francisco: Spinsters Ink

Grewal, S., J. Kay, L. Landor, G. Lewis and P. Parmar (1988) *Charting the Journey*, London: Sheba

Hall-Carpenter Archive (1989) *Inventing Ourselves*, London: Routledge

Hall, R. (1981) *The Unlit Lamp*, London: Virago

Hall, R. (1982) *The Well of Loneliness*, London: Virago

Hanscombe, G. (1983) *Between Friends*, London: Sheba

Hanscombe, G. and Smyers, V. (1987) *Writing for their Lives*, London: Women's Press

Hite, S. *Women and Love*, London: Viking

Holtby, W. (1981) *A Crowded Street*, London: Virago

Holtby, W. (1988) *South Riding*, London: Virago

Hutt, A. (1933) *The Condition of the Working Class in Britain*, London: Martin Lawrence

Hurston, Z. Neale (1986) *Their Eyes were Watching God*, London: Virago

ILEA Afro-Caribbean Language and Literacy Project (1990) *Language and Power*, London: Harcourt Brace Jovanovich

Jeffreys, S. (1990) *anticlimax*, London: Women's Press
Kingston, M. (1977) *China Men*, London: Picador
Kingston, M. (1977) *The Woman Warrior*, London: Picador
Leeds Revolutionary Feminist Group (1981) *Love Your Enemy?* London: Onlywomen
Lefanu, S. (1988) *In the Chinks of the World Machine*, London: Women's Press
Le Guin, U. (1975) *The Dispossessed*, London: Granada
Lesbian History Group (1989) *Not a Passing Phase*, London: Women's Press
LM (1985) *Katherine Mansfield: The Memoirs of LM*, London: Virago
Lorde, A. (1978) *The Black Unicorn*, New York: Norton
Lorde, A. (1984) *Sister Outsider*, Trumansburg: Crossing Press
Lorde, A. (1984) *Zami*, London: Sheba
McEwen, C. (ed.) (1988) *Naming the Waves*, London: Virago
McEwen, C. and S. O'Sullivan, (eds) (1988) *Out the Other Side*, London: Virago
McKluskie, K. (1983) 'Women's Language and Literature: A Problem in Women's Studies' in *Feminist Review* 14
Maitland, S. (1982) *A Map of the New Country*, London: Routledge & Kegan Paul
Manning, R. (1987) *A Corridor of Mirrors*, London: Women's Press
Mansfield, K. (1981) *Collected Short Stories*, Harmondsworth: Penguin
March, C. (1986) *Three Ply Yarn*, London: Women's Press
Marshall, P. (1982) *Brown Girl, Brownstones*, London: Virago
Meulenbelt, A. (1980) *The Shame is Over*, London: Women's Press
Meyers, J. (1978) *Katherine Mansfield*, London: Hamish Hamilton
Millett, K. (1975) *Flying*, London: Paladin
Millett, K. (1977) *Sita*, London: Virago
Moers, E. (1978) *Literary Women*, London: Women's Press
Mohin, L. (ed.) (1979) *One Foot on the Mountain*, London: Onlywomen
Mohin, L. and Shulman, S. (1984) *The Reach*, London: Onlywomen
Molloy, F. (1985) *No Mate for the Magpie*, London: Virago
Montefiore, J. (1983) 'Feminism and the Poetic Tradition' in *Feminist Review* 13
Montefiore, J. (1987) *Feminism and Poetry*, London: Pandora
Morgan, C. (1984) *The Price of Salt*, Tallahassee: Naiad
Morrison, T. (1973) *Sula*, London: Panther
Namjoshi, S. (1981) *Feminist Fables*, London: Sheba
Namjoshi, S. (1985) *Conversations with Cow*, London: Women's Press
Namjoshi, S. (1989) *Because of India*, London: Onlywomen
Nestle, J. (1988) *A Restricted Country*, London: Sheba
Nichols, G. (1983) *I is a Long-Memoried Woman*, London: Karnak House
Nicolson, N. (1974) *Portrait of a Marriage*, London: Futura
Olivia (1966) *Olivia*, Harmondsworth: Penguin
Olsen, T. (1980) *Silences*, London: Virago
Ostriker, A. Suskin (1987) *Stealing the Language*, London: Women's Press
Perkins Gilman, C. (1979) *Herland*, London: Women's Press
Piercy, M. (1976) *Woman on the Edge of Time*, London: Women's Press

Piercy, M. (1983) *Stone, Paper, Knife*, London: Pandora
Plath, S. (1981) *Collected Poems*, London: Faber
Randhawa, R. (1987) *A Wicked Old Woman*, London: Women's Press
Rhys, J. (1968) *Tigers are Better Looking*, Harmondsworth: Penguin
Rich, A. (1974) *Poems: Selected and New*, New York: Norton
Rich, A. (1977) *Of Woman Born*, London: Virago
Rich, A. (1980) *On Lies, Secrets and Silences*, London: Virago
Rich, A. (1984) *The Fact of a Door-Frame*, New York: Norton
Rich, A. (1987) *Blood, Bread and Poetry*, London: Virago
Riley, J. (1985) *The Unbelonging*, London: Women's Press
Riley, J. (1987) *Waiting in the Twilight*, London: Women's Press
Riley, J. (1988) *Romance*, London: Women's Press
Roberts, M. (1978) *A Piece of the Night*, London: Women's Press
Roberts, M. (1983) *The Visitation*, London: Women's Press
Rose, E. Cronan (1980) 'Feminists, Feminism and Writing' in *Women and Writing Newsletter* 3
Rowe, M. (ed.) (1982) *A Spare Rib Reader*, Harmondsworth: Penguin
Sarton, M. (1965) *Mrs Stevenson Hears the Mermaids Singing*, New York: Norton
Sarton, M. (1983) *As We Are Now*, London: Women's Press
Sarton, M. (1984) *A Reckoning*, London: Women's Press
Sarton, M. (1986) *The Magnificent Spinster*, London: Women's Press
Sarton, M. (1990) *The Education of Harriet Hatfield*, London: Women's Press
Segal, L. (1983) 'Sensual Uncertainty' in S. Cartledge and J. Ryan (eds) (1983)
Shan, S. (1985) *In My Own Name*, London: Women's Press
Sheba Collective (eds) (1982) *Everyday Matters 1*, London: Sheba
Sheba Collective (eds) (1984) *Everyday Matters 2*, London: Sheba
Sheba Collective (eds) (1989) *Serious Pleasure*, London: Sheba
Showalter, E. (1977) *A Literature of their Own*, London: Virago
Showalter, E. (ed.) (1986) 'Towards a Feminist Poetics' in *The New Feminist Criticism*, London: Virago
Smith, H. (1987) *Not So Quiet: Step-Daughters of War*, London: Lawrence & Wishart
Smyth, A. (1989) *Wildish Things*, Dublin: Attic Press
Stein, G. (1980) *The Yale Gertrude Stein*, New Haven, Conn.: Yale University Press
Taylor, B. (1983) *Eve and the New Jerusalem*, London: Virago
Thompson, F. (1945) *Lark Rise to Candleford*, Oxford: Oxford University Press
Vance, C. (ed.) (1984) *Pleasure and Danger*, London: Routledge & Kegan Paul
Vivien, R. (1982) *A Woman Appeared to Me*, Tallahassee: Naiad
Walker, A. (1982) *The Color Purple*, London: Women's Press
Walker, A. (1982) *You Can't Keep a Good Woman Down*, London: Women's Press
Walker, A. (1983) 'Only Justice Can Stop a Curse' in Smith, B. (ed.) *Home Girls*, New York: Kitchen Table Press

Walker, A. (1984) *In Love and Trouble*, London: Women's Press
Walker, A. (1984) *In Search of our Mothers' Gardens*, London: Women's Press
Wandor, M. (ed.) (1972) *The Body Politic*, London: Stage 1
Whitman, L. (1982) 'Community Publishing' in *Spare Rib* 115
White, C. (1977) *The Women's Periodical Press in Britain*, London: HMSO
Williamson, J. (1978) *Decoding Advertisements*, London: Boyars
Wilson, A. (1980) *Cactus*, London: Onlywomen
Winship, J. (1987) *Inside Women's Magazines*, London: Pandora
Woolf, V. (1945) *A Room of One's Own*, Harmondsworth: Penguin
Woolf, V. (1950) *Mrs Dalloway*, London: Chatto
Woolf, V. (1977) *Orlando*, London: Panther
Woolf, V. (1977) *Women and Writing*, London: Women's Press
Woolf, V. (1977) *A Writer's Diary*, London: Panther
Woolf, V. (1977) *The Years*, London: Panther

INDEX